THIRD EDITION

TOP NOTCH 2B

ENGLISH FOR TODAY'S WORLD

with Workbook

JOAN SASLOW
ALLEN ASCHER

With *Top Notch Pop* Songs and Karaoke
by Rob Morsberger

Top Notch: English for Today's World   Level 2B with Workbook, Third Edition

Pearson Education, 10 Bank Street, White Plains, NY 10606 USA

Staff credits: The people who made up the *Top Notch* team are Pietro Alongi, Rhea Banker, Peter Benson, Tracey Munz Cataldo, Rosa Chapinal, Aerin Csigay, Dave Dickey, Gina DiLillo, Nancy Flaggman, Irene Frankel, Shelley Gazes, Christopher Leonowicz, Kate McLoughlin, Julie Molnar, Laurie Neaman, Sherri Pemberton, Pamela Pia, Jennifer Raspiller, Charlene Straub, Paula Van Ells, and Kenneth Volcjak.

Cover photo: Sprint/Corbis
Text composition: TSI Graphics

Library of Congress Cataloging-in-Publication Data

Saslow, Joan M.
  Top Notch : English for today's world. Fundamentals / Joan Saslow, Allen Ascher ; With Top Notch Pop Songs
  and Karaoke by Rob Morsberger. — Third Edition.
      pages cm
  Includes biographical references.
  ISBN 978-0-13-354275-2 — ISBN 978-0-13-339348-4 — ISBN 978-0-13-354277-6 — ISBN 978-0-13-354278-3   1. English language—
  Textbooks for foreign speakers. 2. English language—Problems, exercises, etc. 3. English language—Sound recordings for foreign speakers.
  I. Ascher, Allen. II. Morsberger, Robert Eustis, 1929- III. Title. IV. Title: English for today's world.
  PE1128.S2757 2015
  428.2'4--dc23
                    2013044020

Printed in the United States of America
ISBN-10: 0-13-381926-4
ISBN-13: 978-0-13-381926-7
11 2022

pearsonelt.com/topnotch3e

In Memoriam

Rob Morsberger (1959–2013)

The authors wish to acknowledge their memory of and gratitude to **Rob Morsberger**, the gifted composer and songwriter of the *Top Notch Pop* Songs and Karaoke that have provided learners both language practice and pleasure.

Contents

LEARNING OBJECTIVES

	COMMUNICATION GOALS	VOCABULARY	GRAMMAR

UNIT 1
Getting Acquainted
PAGE 2
	• Get reacquainted with someone
	• Greet a visitor to your country
	• Discuss gestures and customs
	• Describe an interesting experience
		• Tourist activities
		• The hand
		• Participial adjectives
			• The present perfect
			  ◦ Statements and <u>yes</u> / <u>no</u> questions
			  ◦ Form and usage
			  ◦ Past participles of irregular verbs
			  ◦ With <u>already</u>, <u>yet</u>, <u>ever</u>, <u>before</u>, and <u>never</u>
			GRAMMAR BOOSTER
			• The present perfect
			  ◦ Information questions
			  ◦ <u>Yet</u> and <u>already</u>: expansion, common errors
			  ◦ <u>Ever</u>, <u>never</u>, and <u>before</u>: use and placement

UNIT 2
Going to the Movies
PAGE 14
	• Apologize for being late
	• Discuss preferences for movie genres
	• Describe and recommend movies
	• Discuss effects of movie violence on viewers
		• Explanations for being late
		• Movie genres
		• Adjectives to describe movies
			• The present perfect
			  ◦ With <u>for</u> and <u>since</u>
			  ◦ Other uses
			• Wants and preferences: <u>would like</u> and <u>would rather</u>
			  ◦ Form and usage
			  ◦ Statements, questions, and answers
			GRAMMAR BOOSTER
			• The present perfect continuous
			• The present participle: spelling
			• Expressing preferences: review, expansion, and common errors

UNIT 3
Staying in Hotels
PAGE 26
	• Leave and take a message
	• Check into a hotel
	• Request housekeeping services
	• Choose a hotel
		• Hotel room types and kinds of beds
		• Hotel room amenities and services
			• The future with <u>will</u>
			  ◦ Form and usage
			  ◦ Statements and questions
			  ◦ Contractions
			• The real conditional
			  ◦ Form and usage
			  ◦ Statements and questions
			GRAMMAR BOOSTER
			• <u>Will</u>: expansion
			• <u>Can</u>, <u>should</u>, and <u>have to</u>: future meaning
			• The real conditinal: factual and future; usage and common errors

UNIT 4
Cars and Driving
PAGE 38
	• Discuss a car accident
	• Describe a car problem
	• Rent a car
	• Discuss good and bad driving
		• Bad driving habits
		• Car parts
		• Ways to respond (with concern / relief)
		• Phrasal verbs for talking about cars
		• Car types
		• Driving behavior
			• The past continuous
			  ◦ Form and usage
			  ◦ Vs. the simple past tense
			• Direct objects with phrasal verbs
			GRAMMAR BOOSTER
			• The past continuous: other uses
			• Nouns and pronouns: review

UNIT 5
Personal Care and Appearance
PAGE 50
	• Ask for something in a store
	• Make an appointment at a salon or spa
	• Discuss ways to improve appearance
	• Define the meaning of beauty
		• Salon services
		• Personal care products
		• Discussing beauty
			• Indefinite quantities and amounts
			  ◦ <u>Some</u> and <u>any</u>
			  ◦ <u>A lot of</u> / <u>lots of</u>, <u>many</u>, and <u>much</u>
			• Indefinite pronouns: <u>someone</u> / <u>no one</u> / <u>anyone</u>
			GRAMMAR BOOSTER
			• <u>Some</u> and <u>any</u>: indefiniteness
			• <u>Too many</u>, <u>too much</u>, and <u>enough</u>
			• Comparative quantifiers <u>fewer</u> and <u>less</u>
			• Indefinite pronouns: <u>something</u>, <u>anything</u>, and <u>nothing</u>

CONVERSATION STRATEGIES	LISTENING / PRONUNCIATION	READING	WRITING
• Use "I don't think so." to soften a negative answer • Say "I know!" to exclaim that you've discovered an answer • Use "Welcome to ____." to greet someone in a new place • Say "That's great." to acknowledge someone's positive experience	**Listening Skills** • Listen to classify • Listen for details **Pronunciation** • Sound reduction in the present perfect	**Texts** • A poster about world customs • A magazine article about non-verbal communication • A travel poster • A photo story **Skills/strategies** • Identify supporting details • Relate to personal experience	**Task** • Write a description of an interesting experience **WRITING BOOSTER** • Avoiding run-on sentences
• Apologize and provide a reason when late • Say "That's fine." to reassure • Offer to repay someone with "How much do I owe?" • Use "What would you rather do . . . ? to ask about preference • Soften a negative response with "To tell you the truth, . . ."	**Listening Skills** • Listen for main ideas • Listen to infer • Dictation **Pronunciation** • Reduction of h	**Texts** • A movie website • Movie reviews • A textbook excerpt about violence in movies • A photo story **Skills/strategies** • Understand from context • Confirm content • Evaluate ideas	**Task** • Write an essay about violence in movies and on TV **WRITING BOOSTER** • Paragraphs • Topic sentences
• Say "Would you like to leave a message?" if someone isn't available • Say "Let's see." to indicate you're checking information • Make a formal, polite request with "May I ____?" • Say "Here you go." when handing someone something • Use "By the way, . . ." to introduce new information	**Listening Skills** • Listen to take phone messages • Listen for main ideas • Listen for details **Pronunciation** • Contractions with <u>will</u>	**Texts** • Phone message slips • A hotel website • A city map • A photo story **Skills/strategies** • Draw conclusions • Identify supporting details • Interpret a map	**Task** • Write a paragraph explaining the reasons for choosing a hotel **WRITING BOOSTER** • Avoiding sentence fragments with <u>because</u> or <u>since</u>
• Express concern about another's condition after an accident • Express relief when hearing all is OK • Use "only" to minimize the seriousness of a situation • Use "actually" to soften negative information • Empathize with "I'm sorry to hear that."	**Listening Skills** • Listen for details • Listen to summarize **Pronunciation** • Stress of particles in phrasal verbs	**Texts** • A questionnaire about bad driving habits • Rental car customer profiles • A feature article about defensive driving • A driving behavior survey • A photo story **Skills/strategies** • Understand from context • Critical thinking	**Task** • Write a paragraph comparing good and bad drivers **WRITING BOOSTER** • Connecting words and sentences: <u>and</u>, <u>in addition</u>, <u>furthermore</u>, and <u>therefore</u>
• Use "Excuse me." to initiate a conversation with a salesperson • Confirm information by repeating it with rising intonation • Use "No problem." to show you don't mind an inconvenience • Use "Let me check" to ask someone to wait while you confirm information	**Listening Skills** • Listen to recognize someone's point of view • Listen to take notes **Pronunciation** • Pronunciation of unstressed vowels	**Texts** • A spa and fitness center advertisement • A health advice column • A photo story **Skills/strategies** • Paraphrase • Understand from context • Confirm content • Apply information	**Task** • Write a letter on how to improve appearance **WRITING BOOSTER** • Writing a formal letter

	COMMUNICATION GOALS	VOCABULARY	GRAMMAR
UNIT 6 **Eating Well** PAGE 62	• Talk about food passions • Make an excuse to decline food • Discuss lifestyle changes • Describe local dishes	• Nutrition terminology • Food passions • Excuses for not eating something • Food descriptions	• <u>Use to</u> / <u>used to</u> • Negative <u>yes</u> / <u>no</u> questions GRAMMAR BOOSTER • <u>Use to</u> / <u>used to</u>: use and form, common errors • <u>Be used to</u> vs. <u>get used to</u> • Repeated actions in the past: <u>would</u> + base form, common errors • Negative <u>yes</u> / <u>no</u> questions: short answers
UNIT 7 **About Personality** PAGE 74	• Get to know a new friend • Cheer someone up • Discuss personality and its origin • Examine the impact of birth order on personality	• Positive and negative adjectives • Terms to discuss psychology and personality	• Gerunds and infinitives • Gerunds as objects of prepositions GRAMMAR BOOSTER • Gerunds and infinitives: other uses • Negative gerunds

UNIT 8
The Arts
PAGE 86
	• Recommend a museum
	• Ask about and describe objects
	• Talk about artistic talent
	• Discuss your favorite artists
		• Kinds of art
		• Adjectives to describe art
		• Objects, handicrafts, and materials
		• Passive participial phrases
			• The passive voice
			  ○ Form, meaning, and usage
			  ○ Statements and questions
			
			GRAMMAR BOOSTER
			• Transitive and intransitive verbs
			• The passive voice: other tenses
			• <u>Yes</u> / <u>no</u> questions in the passive voice: other tenses

UNIT 9
Living in Cyberspace
PAGE 98
	• Troubleshoot a problem
	• Compare product features
	• Describe how you use the Internet
	• Discuss the impact of the Internet
		• Ways to reassure someone
		• The computer screen, components, and commands
		• Internet activities
			• The infinitive of purpose
			• Comparisons with <u>as</u> . . . <u>as</u>
			  ○ Meaning and usage
			  ○ <u>Just</u>, <u>almost</u>, <u>not quite</u>, <u>not nearly</u>
			
			GRAMMAR BOOSTER
			• Expressing purpose with <u>in order to</u> and <u>for</u>
			• <u>As</u> . . . <u>as</u> to compare adverbs
			• Comparatives / superlatives: review
			• Comparison with adverbs

UNIT 10
Ethics and Values
PAGE 110
	• Discuss ethical choices
	• Return someone else's property
	• Express personal values
	• Discuss acts of kindness and honesty
		• Idioms
		• Situations that require an ethical choice
		• Acknowledging thanks
		• Personal values
			• The unreal conditional
			  ○ Form, usage, common errors
			• Possessive pronouns / <u>Whose</u>
			  ○ Form, usage, common errors
			
			GRAMMAR BOOSTER
			• <u>should</u>, <u>ought to</u>, <u>had better</u>
			• <u>have to</u>, <u>must</u>, <u>be supposed to</u>
			• Possessive nouns: review and expansion
			• Pronouns: summary

CONVERSATION STRATEGIES	LISTENING / PRONUNCIATION	READING	WRITING
• Provide an emphatic affirmative response with "Definitely." • Offer food with "Please help yourself." • Acknowledge someone's efforts by saying something positive • Soften the rejection of an offer with "I'll pass on the ___." • Use a negative question to express surprise • Use "It's not a problem." to downplay inconvenience	**Listening Skills** • Listen for details • Listen to personalize **Pronunciation** • Sound reduction: <u>used to</u>	**Texts** • A food guide • Descriptions of types of diets • A magazine article about eating habits • A lifestyle survey • Menu ingredients • A photo story **Skills/strategies** • Understand from context • Summarize • Compare and contrast	**Task** • Write a persuasive paragraph about the differences in present-day and past diets **WRITING BOOSTER** • Connecting ideas: subordinating conjunctions
• Clarify an earlier question with "Well, for example, . . ." • Buy time to think with "Let's see." • Use auxiliary <u>do</u> to emphasize a verb • Thank someone for showing interest. • Offer empathy with "I know what you mean."	**Listening Skills** • Listen for main ideas • Listen for specific information • Classify information • Infer information **Pronunciation** • Reduction of <u>to</u> in infinitives	**Texts** • A pop psychology website • A textbook excerpt about the nature / nurture controversy • Personality surveys • A photo story **Skills/strategies** • Understand vocabulary from context • Make personal comparisons	**Task** • Write an essay describing someone's personality **WRITING BOOSTER** • Parallel structure
• Say "Be sure not to miss ___." to emphasize the importance of an action • Introduce the first aspect of an opinion with "For one thing, . . ." • Express enthusiasm for what someone has said with "No kidding!" • Invite someone's opinion with "What do you think of ___?"	**Listening Skills** • Understand from context • Listen to take notes • Infer point of view **Pronunciation** • Emphatic stress	**Texts** • Museum descriptions • A book excerpt about the origin of artistic talent • An artistic survey • A photo story **Skills/strategies** • Recognize the main idea • Identify supporting details • Paraphrase	**Task** • Write a detailed description of a decorative object **WRITING BOOSTER** • Providing supporting details
• Ask for assistance with "Could you take a look at ___?" • Introduce an explanation with "Well, . . ." • Make a suggestion with "Why don't you try ___ing?" • Express interest informally with "Oh, yeah?" • Use "Everyone says . . ." to introduce a popular opinion • Say "Well, I've heard ___." to support a point of view	**Listening Skills** • Listen for the main idea • Listen for details **Pronunciation** • Stress in <u>as</u> . . . <u>as</u> phrases	**Texts** • A social network website • An internet user survey • Newspaper clippings about the Internet • A photo story **Skills/strategies** • Understand from context • Relate to personal experience	**Task** • Write an essay evaluating the benefits and problems of the Internet **WRITING BOOSTER** • Organizing ideas
• Say "You think so?" to reconfirm someone's opinion • Provide an emphatic affirmative response with "Absolutely." • Acknowledge thanks with "Don't mention it."	**Listening Skills** • Listen to infer information • Listen for main ideas • Understand vocabulary from context • Support ideas with details **Pronunciation** • Blending of <u>d</u> + <u>y</u> in <u>would you</u>	**Texts** • A personal values self-test • Print and online news stories about kindness and honesty • A photo story **Skills/strategies** • Summarize • Interpret information • Relate to personal experience	**Task** • Write an essay about someone's personal choice **WRITING BOOSTER** • Introducing conflicting ideas: <u>On the one hand</u>; <u>On the other hand</u>

TO THE TEACHER

What is *Top Notch?* *Top Notch* is a six-level* communicative course that prepares adults and young adults to interact successfully and confidently with both native and non-native speakers of English.

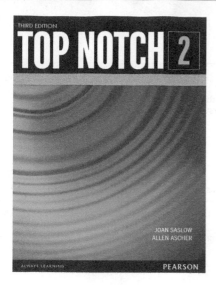

The goal of *Top Notch* is to make English unforgettable through:

- Multiple exposures to new language
- Numerous opportunities to practice it
- Deliberate and intensive recycling

The *Top Notch* course has two beginning levels—*Top Notch Fundamentals* for true beginners and *Top Notch 1* for false beginners. *Top Notch* is benchmarked to the Global Scale of English and is tightly correlated to the Can-do Statements of the Common European Framework of Reference.

Each full level of *Top Notch* contains material for 60–90 hours of classroom instruction. In addition, the entire course can be tailored to blended learning with an integrated online component, *MyEnglishLab.*

NEW This third edition of *Top Notch* includes these new features: Extra Grammar Exercises, digital full-color Vocabulary Flash Cards, Conversation Activator videos, and Pronunciation Coach videos.

* *Summit 1* and *Summit 2* are the titles of the 5th and 6th levels of the *Top Notch* course.

Award-Winning Instructional Design*

Daily confirmation of progress

Each easy-to-follow two-page lesson begins with a clearly stated practical communication goal closely aligned to the Common European Framework's Can-do Statements. All activities are integrated with the goal, giving vocabulary and grammar meaning and purpose. *Now You Can* activities ensure that students achieve each goal and confirm their progress in every class session.

Explicit vocabulary and grammar

Clear captioned picture-dictionary illustrations with accompanying audio take the guesswork out of meaning and pronunciation. Grammar presentations containing both rules and examples clarify form, meaning, and use. The unique *Recycle this Language* feature continually puts known words and grammar in front of students' eyes as they communicate, to make sure language remains active.

High-frequency social language

Twenty memorable conversation models provide appealing natural social language that students can carry "in their pockets" for use in real life. Rigorous controlled and free discussion activities systematically stimulate recycling of social language, ensuring that it's not forgotten.

Linguistic and cultural fluency

Top Notch equips students to interact with people from different language backgrounds by including authentic accents on the audio. Conversation Models, Photo Stories, and cultural fluency activities prepare students for social interactions in English with people from unfamiliar cultures.

Active listening syllabus

All Vocabulary presentations, Pronunciation presentations, Conversation Models, Photo Stories, Listening Comprehension exercises, and Readings are recorded on the audio to help students develop good pronunciation, intonation, and auditory memory. In addition, approximately fifty carefully developed listening tasks at each level of *Top Notch* develop crucial listening comprehension skills such as listen for details, listen for main ideas, listen to activate vocabulary, listen to activate grammar, and listen to confirm information.

*We wish you and your students enjoyment and success with **Top Notch 2.** We wrote it for you.*

Joan Saslow and Allen Ascher

* *Top Notch* is the recipient of the Association of Educational Publishers' *Distinguished Achievement Award.*

ActiveTeach

Maximize the impact of your *Top Notch* lessons. This digital tool provides an interactive classroom experience that can be used with or without an interactive whiteboard (IWB). It includes a full array of digital and printable features.

For class presentation . . .

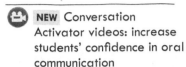 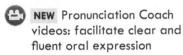 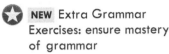 

- **NEW** Conversation Activator videos: increase students' confidence in oral communication

- **NEW** Pronunciation Coach videos: facilitate clear and fluent oral expression

- **NEW** Extra Grammar Exercises: ensure mastery of grammar

- **NEW** Digital Full-Color Vocabulary Flash Cards: accelerate retention of new vocabulary

PLUS

- Clickable Audio: instant access to the complete classroom audio program
- *Top Notch TV* Video Program: a hilarious sitcom and authentic on-the-street interviews
- *Top Notch Pop* Songs and Karaoke: original songs for additional language practice

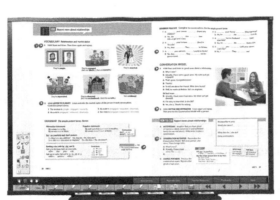

For planning . . .

- A *Methods Handbook* for a communicative classroom
- Detailed timed lesson plans for each two-page lesson
- *Top Notch TV* teaching notes
- Complete answer keys, audio scripts, and video scripts

For extra support . . .

- Hundreds of extra printable activities, with teaching notes
- *Top Notch Pop* language exercises
- *Top Notch TV* activity worksheets

For assessment . . .

- Ready-made unit and review achievement tests with options to edit, add, or delete items.

MyEnglishLab

An optional online learning tool

- **NEW** Grammar Coach videos, plus the Pronunciation Coach videos, and Digital Vocabulary Flash Cards
- **NEW** Immediate and meaningful feedback on wrong answers
- **NEW** Remedial grammar exercises
- Interactive practice of all material presented in the course
- Grade reports that display performance and time on task
- Auto-graded achievement tests

Workbook

Lesson-by-lesson written exercises to accompany the Student's Book

Full-Course Placement Tests

Choose printable or online version

Classroom Audio Program

- A set of Audio CDs, as an alternative to the clickable audio in the ActiveTeach
- Contains a variety of authentic regional and non-native accents to build comprehension of diverse English speakers
- **NEW** The entire audio program is available for students at www.english.com/topnotch3e. The mobile app *Top Notch Go* allows access anytime, anywhere and lets students practice at their own pace.

Teacher's Edition and Lesson Planner

- Detailed interleaved lesson plans, language and culture notes, answer keys, and more
- Also accessible in digital form in the ActiveTeach

For more information: www.pearsonelt.com/topnotch3e

UNIT 6 Eating Well

PREVIEW

COMMUNICATION GOALS
1 Talk about food passions.
2 Make an excuse to decline food.
3 Discuss lifestyle changes.
4 Describe local dishes.

A HEALTHY DIET
The right balance of foods will keep you healthy.

FATS, OILS, SWEETS — eat rarely

DAIRY — 2-3 servings per day for calcium

FRUIT — 2-4 servings per day for vitamins and fiber

VEGETABLES — 3-5 servings per day for vitamins and fiber

BREAD, GRAINS, PASTA — 6-11 servings per day for carbohydrates

MEAT, FISH, BEANS — 2-3 servings per day for protein and vitamins

▶ 3:19 **VOCABULARY**

Calcium: Dairy products and leafy green vegetables provide calcium for healthy bones and teeth.

Carbohydrates: Grains, pasta, and bread are sources of healthy carbohydrates.

Protein: Meat, fish, poultry, eggs, legumes, and nuts are rich sources of protein.

Vitamins: Vitamins A, B, C, and D come from a variety of foods, and they are important for good health.

A Look at the suggestions above for eating a healthy diet. Do you think this diet is healthy? Why or why not?

B Complete the chart about the foods you eat each day. Compare charts with a partner.

C **DISCUSSION** How are the Healthy Diet suggestions different from your chart? Which do you think is a healthier diet? Explain.

2–3 servings a day
3–5 servings a day
More than 5 servings a day

D ▶ 3:20 **PHOTO STORY** Read and listen to people talking about food choices.

Rita: Didn't you tell me you were avoiding sweets?

Joy: I couldn't resist! I had a craving for chocolate.

Rita: Well, I have to admit it looks pretty good. How many calories are in that thing anyway?

Joy: I have no idea. Want to try some?

Rita: Thanks. But I think I'd better pass. I'm avoiding carbs.*

Joy: You? I don't believe it. You never used to turn down chocolate!

Rita: I know. But I'm watching my weight now.

Joy: Come on! It's really good.

Rita: OK. Maybe just a bite.

Joy: Hey, you only live once!

*carbs (informal) = carbohydrates

E **FOCUS ON LANGUAGE** Find an underlined sentence or phrase in the Photo Story with the same meaning as each of the following.

1 I don't know. ....
2 I should say no. ....
3 I couldn't stop myself. ....
4 I'm trying not to get heavier. ....

5 I really wanted . . . .
6 I agree . . . .
7 say no to ....
8 I'll try a little. ....

SPEAKING

Read the descriptions of diets. Would you ever try any of them? Why or why not?

> ❝ I don't believe in the Atkins Diet. A lot of meat, eggs, and cheese doesn't sound like the right balance of foods for good health. ❞

The Mushroom Diet
For weight loss.
Replace lunch or dinner every day—for two weeks—with a mushroom dish.

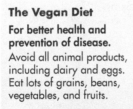

The Vegan Diet
For better health and prevention of disease.
Avoid all animal products, including dairy and eggs. Eat lots of grains, beans, vegetables, and fruits.

The Atkins Diet
For weight loss.
Eat high-protein foods such as meat, eggs, and cheese. Avoid foods that are high in carbohydrates, such as potatoes, bread, grains, and sugar.

The Juice Fast
For better health and prevention of disease.
Instead of food, drink four to six glasses of fresh vegetable and fruit juices for anywhere from three days to three weeks. Get plenty of rest and avoid exercise during the fast.

VOCABULARY *Food passions*

A ▶3:21 Read and listen. Then listen again and repeat.

I'm **crazy about** seafood.
I'm **a big** meat **eater**.
I'm **a big** coffee **drinker**.
I'm **a chocolate addict**.
I'm **a pizza lover**.

I **can't stand** fish.
I'm **not crazy about** chocolate.
I **don't care for** steak.
I'm **not much of a pizza eater**.
I'm **not much of a coffee drinker**.

B ▶3:22 **LISTEN TO ACTIVATE VOCABULARY** Circle the correct words to complete each statement about the speakers' food passions.

1 She (is crazy about / doesn't care for) sushi.

2 He (loves / can't stand) asparagus.

3 She (is a mango lover / doesn't care for mangoes).

4 He (is a big pasta eater / isn't crazy about pasta).

5 She (is an ice cream addict / can't stand ice cream).

sushi

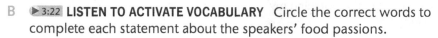

mangoes   **pasta**   **ice cream**   **asparagus**

C **PAIR WORK** Tell your partner about some of your food passions.

> ❝ I'm really a seafood lover, but I'm not crazy about clams. ❞

GRAMMAR *Use to / used to*

Use use to and used to + the base form of a verb to describe things that were true in the past but are no longer true in the present.

I used to be crazy about candy, but now I don't care for it.
She didn't use to eat cheese, but now she has it all the time.

Did you use to eat a lot of fatty foods? | Yes, I did. | OR | Yes, I used to.
                                         | No, I didn't. | | No, I didn't use to.

What did you use to have for breakfast? (Eggs and sausage. But not anymore.)
Why did you use to eat so much? (Because I didn't use to worry about my health.)

Be careful!

They **used** to . . . BUT | They didn't **use** to . . .
                          | Did they **use** to . . . ?

GRAMMAR BOOSTER p. 134
• Use to / used to: use and form, common errors
• Be used to vs. get used to
• Repeated actions in the past: would + base form, common errors

GRAMMAR PRACTICE Use the context to help you complete each sentence with <u>used to</u> or <u>didn't use to</u>. Then write two sentences about yourself.

1 Gary .... go out to eat a lot, but now he eats at home more often.

2 Nina .... eat a lot of pasta, but now she does.

3 Vinnie .... drink a lot of coffee, but now he's a coffee addict.

4 Anton .... eat a lot of vegetables, but now he doesn't.

5 Cate .... hate seafood, but now she's crazy about fish.

6 Ted .... eat a lot of fatty foods, but now he avoids them.

7 Burt .... drink a lot of water, but now he has several glasses a day.

8 May .... like salad, but now she has salads several times a week.

9 (used to) I ....
....

10 (didn't use to) I ....
....

DIGITAL
MORE
EXERCISES

DIGITAL
VIDEO
COACH

PRONUNCIATION *Sound reduction: <u>used to</u>*

▶ 3:23 Notice how the pronunciation of <u>to</u> in <u>used to</u> changes to /tə/ in natural speech. Read and listen. Then listen again and repeat. Practice the sentences on your own.

1 I used to be a big meat eater.

2 Jack used to like sweets.

3 Sally used to be crazy about fries.

4 They didn't use to like seafood.

CONVERSATION MODEL

A ▶ 3:24 Read and listen to two people talking about their food passions.

A: Are you a big coffee drinker?

B: Definitely. I'm crazy about coffee. What about you?

A: I used to drink it a lot. But recently I've cut back.

B: Well, I couldn't live without it.

B ▶ 3:25 **RHYTHM AND INTONATION** Listen again and repeat. Then practice the Conversation Model with a partner.

NOW YOU CAN Talk about food passions

A **NOTEPADDING** Complete the notepad with foods you like and dislike.

DIGITAL
VIDEO B **CONVERSATION ACTIVATOR** With a partner, change the Conversation Model, exchanging information about your food passions. Talk about what you used to and didn't use to eat or drink. Use your notepad and the Vocabulary from page 64.

A: Are you a big .... ?
B: .... What about you?
A: ....

DON'T STOP!
• Ask about more foods and drinks.

My food passions	
Foods I'm crazy about	Foods I can't stand

C **CHANGE PARTNERS** Talk about other food passions.

GOAL Make an excuse to decline food

CONVERSATION MODEL

A ▶3:26 Read and listen to a dinner guest make an excuse to decline food.

A: Please help yourself.

B: Everything looks great! But I'll pass on the chicken.

A: Don't you eat chicken?

B: Actually, no. I'm a vegetarian.

A: I'm sorry. I didn't know that.

B: It's not a problem. I'll have something else.

B ▶3:27 **RHYTHM AND INTONATION** Listen again and repeat. Then practice the Conversation Model with a partner.

▶3:28 **Variations**
It's not a problem.
Don't worry.
I'm fine.

VOCABULARY *Excuses for not eating something*

DIGITAL FLASH CARDS

A ▶3:29 Read and listen. Then listen again and repeat.

Coffee **doesn't agree with me**.

I'm **on a diet**. / I'm **trying to lose weight**.

I don't eat beef. It's **against my religion**.

I'm **allergic to** chocolate.

I'm **avoiding** sugar.

I **don't care for** broccoli.

B ▶3:30 **LISTEN TO ACTIVATE VOCABULARY** Listen to each conversation. Write the letter to complete each statement. Then listen again to check your work.

.... **1** Cindy . . .   **a** is a vegetarian.

.... **2** Frankie . . .   **b** is avoiding fatty, salty foods.

.... **3** Marie . . .   **c** is trying to lose weight.

.... **4** Susan . . .   **d** is allergic to something.

.... **5** George . . .   **e** doesn't care for seafood.

C **PAIR WORK** Talk about foods or drinks you avoid. Explain why.

" I usually don't eat fried foods. I'm trying to lose weight. "

GRAMMAR *Negative <u>yes</u> / <u>no</u> questions*

Use negative <u>yes</u> / <u>no</u> questions . . .
- **to confirm information you think is true.**
  <u>Isn't</u> Jane a vegetarian? (Yes, she is.)
  <u>Didn't</u> he go on a diet last week? (Yes. He's trying the Atkins Diet.)
- **when you want someone to agree with you.**
  <u>Don't</u> you love Italian food? (Yes, it's delicious!)
  <u>Wasn't</u> that a terrible dinner? (Actually, no. I thought it was good.)
- **to express surprise.**
  <u>Aren't</u> you going to have cake? (I'm sorry, but I'm on a diet.)
  <u>Hasn't</u> he tried the chicken? (No. He's a vegetarian.)

> **GRAMMAR BOOSTER** p. 135
> - Negative <u>yes</u> / <u>no</u> questions: short answers

GRAMMAR PRACTICE Complete each negative <u>yes</u> / <u>no</u> question.

1 A: .... you allergic to tomatoes?
  B: Me? No. You're thinking of my brother.

2 A: .... that lunch yesterday delicious?
  B: It was fantastic!

3 A: .... we already have steak this week?
  B: Yes, we did.

4 A: .... your husband been on a diet?
  B: Yes. But it's driving him crazy.

5 A: .... asparagus disgusting?
  B: Actually, I like it.

6 A: .... you like your pasta?
  B: Actually, it was a little too spicy for me.

NOW YOU CAN Make an excuse to decline food

A **NOTEPADDING** Look at the photos. On a separate sheet of paper, use the Vocabulary to write an excuse to decline each food.

B **CONVERSATION ACTIVATOR** With a partner, change the Conversation Model to role-play a dinner conversation. Use the photos to offer foods. Use your notepad to make excuses to decline that food. Then change roles. OPTION: Role-play a dinner conversation with more than one classmate.

A: Please help yourself.
B: Everything looks .... ! But I'll pass on the ....
A: Don't you eat .... ?
B: Actually, ...
A: I'm sorry. I didn't know that.
B: .... I'll have ....

DON'T STOP!
- Offer drinks and other foods.
- Talk about food passions.

RECYCLE THIS LANGUAGE.

be crazy about __	can't stand __
be a big __ eater / drinker	be not crazy about __
be a(n) __ addict / lover	not care for __

C **CHANGE PARTNERS** Practice the conversation again.

octopus   shellfish

tofu   steak

broccoli   beets

chocolate

BEFORE YOU READ

EXPLORE YOUR IDEAS Do you think people's eating habits are better or worse than they used to be? Explain with examples.

READING ▶ 3:31

How Can It Be?
Americans gain weight . . . while the French stay thin

Have you ever wondered why Americans struggle with watching their weight, while the French, who consume all that rich food—the bread, the cheese, the wine, and the heavy sauces—continue to stay thin? Now a report from Cornell University suggests a possible answer. A study of almost 300 participants from France and the U.S. provides clues about how lifestyle and decisions about eating may affect weight. Researchers concluded that the French tend to stop eating when they feel full. However, Americans tend to stop when their plate is completely empty, or they have reached the end of their favorite TV show.

According to Dr. Joseph Mercola, who writes extensively about health issues, the French see eating as an important part of their lifestyle. They enjoy food and, therefore, spend a fairly long time at the table. In contrast, Americans see eating as something to do quickly as they squeeze meals between the other activities of the day. Mercola believes Americans have lost the ability to sense when they are actually full. So they keep eating long after the French would have stopped. In addition, he argues that, by tradition, the French tend to shop daily, walking to small shops and farmers' markets where they have a choice of fresh fruits, vegetables, and eggs as well as high-quality meats and cheeses for each meal. In contrast, Americans tend to drive their cars to huge supermarkets to buy canned and frozen foods for the whole week.

Despite all these differences, new reports show that recent lifestyle changes may be affecting French eating habits. Today, the rate of obesity—or extreme overweight—among adults is only 6%. However, as American fast-food restaurants gain acceptance, and the young turn their backs on older traditions, the obesity rate among French children has reached 17%—and is growing.

A **UNDERSTAND FROM CONTEXT** Use the context of the article to help you choose the same meaning as each underlined word or phrase.

1 Have you ever wondered why Americans <u>struggle with</u> watching their weight . . .

    a have an easy time   **b** have a difficult time   **c** don't care about

2 . . . while the French, who consume all that <u>rich food</u>, ...

    a fatty, high-calorie food   **b** low-fat, low-calorie food   **c** expensive food

3 . . . continue to <u>stay thin</u>?

    a worry about their weight   **b** not become overweight   **c** gain weight

4 Researchers concluded that the French tend to stop eating when they feel <u>full</u>.

    a like they can't eat any more   **b** worried about their weight   **c** hungry

5 . . . the French see eating as an important part of their <u>lifestyle</u>.

    a personal care and appearance   **b** culture or daily routine   **c** meals

B **SUMMARIZE** According to the article, why do the French stay thin while Americans gain weight? Write a four-sentence summary of the Reading. Then share your summary with the class.

> Compared to Americans, the French stay thin because . . .

C **COMPARE AND CONTRAST** In your country, do people generally stay thin or do they struggle with watching their weight? Are lifestyles in your country closer to those of France or the U.S., as described in the article?

DIGITAL
MORE
RCISES

> " I think people here are more like people in France. They like to eat, but they don't gain weight easily. "

NOW YOU CAN Discuss lifestyle changes

A **FRAME YOUR IDEAS** Complete the lifestyle self-assessment.

1 Have you ever changed the way you eat in order to lose weight? ● yes ● no

If so, what have you done?
○ ate less food
○ cut back on desserts
○ avoided fatty foods
○ other (explain) _____

Were you successful? ○ yes ○ no
Why or why not? Explain. _____
_____

2 Have you ever changed the way you eat in order to avoid illness? ● yes ● no

If so, what changes have you made?
○ stopped eating fast foods
○ started eating whole grains
○ started eating more vegetables
○ other (explain) _____

Were you successful? ○ yes ○ no
Why or why not? Explain. _____
_____

3 Have you ever tried to lead a more active lifestyle? ● yes ● no

If so, what have you done?
○ started working out in a gym
○ started running or walking
○ started playing sports
○ other (explain) _____

Were you successful? ○ yes ○ no
Why or why not? Explain. _____
_____

B **CLASS SURVEY** On the board, summarize your class's lifestyles.

How many students . . .
- want to make some lifestyle changes?
- have gone on a diet to lose weight?
- have changed their diet to improve their health?
- have been successful with a diet?
- lead an active lifestyle?

C **DISCUSSION** How do you think your classmates compare to most people in your country? Are they generally healthier or less healthy? What do you think people need to do to have a healthy lifestyle?

> " I think my classmates are healthier than most people in this country. Too many people eat fast foods. They need to eat healthier food and exercise more. "

Text-mining (optional)
Find and underline three words or phrases in the Reading that were new to you. Use them in your Discussion.
For example: "gain weight."

GOAL Describe local dishes

BEFORE YOU LISTEN

A ▶3:32 **VOCABULARY** • *Food descriptions* Read and listen. Then listen again and repeat.

It looks terrific.

It smells terrible.

It tastes { sweet. / spicy. / salty. / sour.

It smells like / **It tastes like** / **It looks like** } chicken.

It's { soft. / hard.

It's { chewy. / crunchy.

B **PAIR WORK** Use the Vocabulary to describe foods you know.

" Apples are crunchy. "

LISTENING COMPREHENSION

A ▶3:33 **LISTEN FOR DETAILS** First, listen to the descriptions of foods from around the world and write the letter of each food. Then listen again and choose the Vocabulary that completes each description.

...*c*.... **1** It's (crunchy / chewy / hard), and it tastes (salty / sweet / sour).

.... **2** It tastes (salty / sweet / spicy), and it's (soft / hard / crunchy).

.... **3** It's (soft / chewy / crunchy), and it tastes (salty / sweet / spicy).

.... **4** It tastes (salty / sweet / spicy). Some think it (tastes / smells / looks) awful.

.... **5** It (smells / tastes / looks) great, and it (smells / tastes / looks) awful.

.... **6** They're (crunchy / chewy / hard), and they taste (salty / sweet / spicy).

f

kim chee / Korea **cabbage**

e

caviar / Russia

a

grasshopper

chapulines / Mexico

b

cho dofu / China

c

mochi / Japan

d

Jell-O ® / United States

B   ▶ 3:34 **LISTEN TO PERSONALIZE**   Listen again. After each food, discuss with
a partner whether you would like to try that food. Explain why or why not.

Describe local dishes

A   **FRAME YOUR IDEAS**   Choose three local dishes that you would
recommend to a visitor to your country. Write notes about each.

Name of dish:
Rain doughnuts

Description:
soft and sweet

What's in it?
flour, eggs, milk

Name of dish:

Description:

What's in it?

☐1

Name of dish:

Description:

What's in it?

☐3

Name of dish:

Description:

What's in it?

☐2

B   **PAIR WORK**   Role-play a conversation in which one of you is a visitor
to your country. Introduce and describe your dishes to the "visitor."
Use the Vocabulary. For example:

❝ Have you tried rain doughnuts? ❞

❝ No, I haven't. What are they like? ❞

❝ Well, they're soft. And they taste sweet . . . ❞

"rain doughnuts" / Brazil

🔄 **RECYCLE THIS LANGUAGE.**

Ask about the dish	Comment on the dish	
What's in [it / them]?	It sounds / they sound [great].	I'm allergic to __.
Is it / Are they [spicy / sweet]?	I'm crazy about __.	I'm avoiding __.
How do you make [it / them]?	I'm a big __ eater.	__ [don't / doesn't] agree with me.
Is it / Are they [popular]?	I'm a(n) __ [addict / lover].	__ [is / are] against my religion.
Does it / Do they taste [salty]?	I [used to / didn't use to] eat __.	I'm not much of a __ [eater].
	I don't care for __.	I'm [on a diet / trying to lose weight].

A ▶ 3:35 Listen to the conversation in a restaurant. Cross out the foods that the speakers don't mention.

beef and broccoli	chicken	clams	noodles	pasta
pizza	salmon	scallops	shrimp	steak

B ▶ 3:36 Now listen again and complete the statements.

The man doesn't care for ....

He would rather eat ....

C Complete the negative <u>yes</u> / <u>no</u> question for each situation.

1 The weather today is sunny and beautiful. You turn to your friend and say: "................ the weather fantastic?"

2 You've just finished dinner. It was a terrible meal. As you leave, you say to your friend: "................ that meal awful?"

3 You're sightseeing in China. From your tour bus window you see a long wall in the distance. You say to the person sitting next to you: "................ that the Great Wall?"

4 You're surprised to see your friend eating breakfast at 11:30. You say: "................ you .... breakfast yet?"

5 You see a woman on the street. You're pretty sure it's Norah Jones, the singer. You go up to her and ask: "................ you Norah Jones?"

D Write five sentences about things you used to or didn't use to do or think when you were younger. For example:

> I didn't use to like coffee when I was younger.

E Write short descriptions of the following foods.

apples	bananas	carrots	grapefruit
ice cream	onions	squid	steak

> Carrots are orange, and they're sweet and crunchy.

For additional language practice . . .

♫ TOP NOTCH **POP** • Lyrics p. 154
"A Perfect Dish"

[DIGITAL SONG] [DIGITAL KARAOKE]

WRITING

Write a paragraph on the following topic: Do you think people are eating healthier or less healthy foods than they used to? Give examples to support your opinion.

> I think people are eating a lot of unhealthy foods today.
>
> People used to eat a lot of fresh foods. However, lately . . .

WRITING BOOSTER p. 148
• Connecting ideas: subordinating conjunctions
• Guidance for this writing exercise

International Buffet
Today's Selections

Pad Thai • Thailand

Ingredients: rice noodles, tofu, peanuts, fish sauce, sugar, lime juice, vegetable oil, garlic, shrimp, eggs, hot peppers

Bi Bim Bop • Korea

Ingredients: rice, beef, soy sauce, sesame oil, garlic, black pepper, salt, eggs, lettuce, rice wine, hot peppers

Chicken Mole • Mexico

Ingredients: chicken, salt, vegetable oil, onions, garlic, tomatoes, chocolate, hot peppers

Potato Soup • Colombia

Ingredients: chicken, three kinds of potatoes, corn, avocados

Tabouleh Salad • Lebanon

Ingredients: parsley, mint, onions, tomatoes, salt, black pepper, cracked wheat, lemon juice, olive oil

Pot Stickers • China

Ingredients: flour, cabbage, pork, green onions, sesame oil, salt

Stuffed Rocoto Peppers • Peru

Ingredients: onions, garlic, ground beef, hard-boiled eggs, raisins, cheese, rocoto peppers, vegetable oil

ORAL REVIEW

CHALLENGE Choose a dish and study the photo and the ingredients for one minute. Then close your book. Describe the dish.

PAIR WORK

1 Create a conversation for the man and woman in which they look at the foods and talk about their food passions. For example:
Have you tried Pad Thai? It's terrific!

2 Create a conversation in which the man or the woman suggests and offers foods. The other makes excuses. Start like this:
A: *Would you like some __?*
B: *Actually, __.*

3 Choose a dish and create a conversation between someone from that country and a visitor. For example:
Have you ever tried __?

NOW I CAN

☐ Talk about food passions.
☐ Make an excuse to decline food.
☐ Discuss lifestyle changes.
☐ Describe local dishes.

COMMUNICATION GOALS
1 Get to know a new friend.
2 Cheer someone up.
3 Discuss personality and its origin.
4 Examine the impact of birth order.

PREVIEW

The **Psychology** of Color

According to research, colors have a powerful effect on us. Take the test and then see if your answers are confirmed by the research. You may be surprised! (Check your answers below.)

Color test

1) What color is the most attention-getting?

● black   ○ yellow   ● red   ○ other

2) What color is most likely to make people feel angry?

● black   ○ yellow   ● pink   ○ other

3) What color is best for a hospital room?

○ pink   ○ white   ● green   ○ other

4) What color often makes people feel tired?

○ green   ● blue   ● pink   ○ other

5) What is the least appealing color for food?

● black   ○ yellow   ● blue   ○ other

Answers

1) Experts say red attracts the most attention. Using red for traffic lights and warning lights makes them more noticeable.
2) Studies have shown that being in a yellow room makes it more likely for adults to lose their tempers and for babies to cry.
3) Green is the easiest color on the eye, and it causes people to relax. Painting a hospital room green helps patients get the rest they need.
4) Research has shown that looking at pink can cause people to feel tired. Some sports teams have painted the dressing room of the opposing team pink to reduce the players' energy.
5) Researchers in marketing have found that using blue in processed foods is unappealing. They believe that this is because blue is rare in nature. Painting a restaurant red, on the other hand, increases the appetite. Many restaurants are painted red.

Questionnaire

What are your color preferences?
Look at the colors below.

YELLOW-GREEN
EMERALD GREEN
BRIGHT ORANGE
DARK GRAY
LIGHT BLUE
TOMATO RED
LILAC

Which color do you find the most appealing? _____

Which color do you most associate with happiness? _____

Which color do you most associate with being sad? _____

A **CLASS SURVEY** How many classmates answered the questions on the test correctly? Which color on the questionnaire was the most appealing to your classmates?

B **DISCUSSION** In your opinion, what makes people like some colors and dislike others?

" I think people like colors that remind them of things they like. "

" I agree. I love blue. It reminds me of the sky. I love being outdoors. "

C ▶4:02 **PHOTO STORY** Read and listen to a couple talking about what color to repaint their living room.

Chelsea: You know what? I'm getting a little tired of looking at this wallpaper.

Chad: Well, maybe it's time for a change. What would you think about getting the room painted? I never loved that wallpaper, anyway.

Chelsea: Actually, I don't think either of us did. We only got it because we couldn't agree on a paint color.

Chad: Oh, yeah. Now I remember. You wanted pink, and I said it was too feminine.

Chelsea: Actually, I never thought it was pink. To me it was a soft rose.

Chad: Well, what would you say to a nice blue?

Chelsea: Blue? *Way* too masculine.

Chad: *What?!*

Chelsea: I'm just pulling your leg, silly! Blue would be great.

Later that day

Chad: This one's nice—very relaxing.

Chelsea: True, but I'm not sure the furniture would go with it.

Chad: Good point. I'd hate to have to get all new stuff . . . You know, maybe we're on the wrong track.

Chelsea: What do you mean?

Chad: All of a sudden, I'm thinking white. It's classic, and . . .

Chelsea: And it goes with everything!

D **PARAPHRASE** Restate the expressions from the Photo Story in your own way.

1 "I'm just pulling your leg."

2 "I'm not sure the furniture would go with it."

3 "Good point."

4 "Maybe we're on the wrong track."

E **THINK AND EXPLAIN** All the statements are false. Explain how you know they are false.

1 Chelsea still likes the wallpaper.

> 66 Chelsea says, 'I'm getting a little tired of looking at this wallpaper.' 99

2 Chelsea didn't want a rose-colored living room.

3 Chelsea truly thinks that blue is too masculine.

4 Chelsea thinks the blue Chad likes would go nicely with the furniture.

5 Chad would like to buy new furniture.

6 It's Chelsea's idea to paint the living room white.

7 They agree the furniture wouldn't go with white.

SPEAKING

Choose colors for rooms. Use the Color Test for ideas. Compare charts and reasons with a partner.

Room	Color	Your reason
a bedroom for a married couple		
a bedroom for a teenaged girl		
a bedroom for a 10-year-old boy		
a kitchen		
a family living room		

GOAL Get to know a new friend

GRAMMAR *Gerunds and infinitives*

Gerunds and infinitives come from verb forms but function as nouns in a sentence, often as direct objects.

Gerund = an **-ing** form of a verb
She enjoys painting.

Infinitive = **to** + a base form
He wants to paint the kitchen yellow.

Use a gerund after the following verbs and expressions: avoid, discuss, dislike, don't mind, enjoy, feel like, practice, quit, suggest

Use an infinitive after the following verbs and expressions: agree, be sure, choose, decide, expect, hope, learn, need, plan, seem, want, wish, would like

Other verbs and expressions can be followed by either a gerund or an infinitive: begin, can't stand, continue, hate, like, love, prefer, start

Remember: There are two other -ing forms:
She is **painting**. (present participle)
The trip was **relaxing**. (participial adjective)

GRAMMAR BOOSTER p. 136
• Gerunds and infinitives: usage within sentences

A **GRAMMAR PRACTICE** Complete the suggestions for ways to make new friends, using the verbs plus gerund or infinitive direct objects.

FIVE WAYS TO MAKE NEW FRIENDS

Everyone .... friends. We .... these principles:
1 want / make   2 suggest / follow

1. .... friendly to everyone you meet. Take advantage of every opportunity.
3 decide / be

2. Even if you .... , ... interest in at least one new person
4 not feel like / socialize   5 learn / show
every day. .... every new acquaintance .... a real friend, but if you
6 not expect   7 become
.... new friends, this is a good way to start.
8 would like / meet

3. .... new acquaintances questions about themselves. People ....
9 be sure / ask   10 enjoy / talk
about themselves.

4. .... too much about yourself. .... people questions about their
11 avoid / talk   12 practice / ask
interests and opinions before you .... them about your own.
13 begin / tell

5. If you .... later, ... something that you both like. If your new friend
14 decide / get together   15 plan / do
has different interests from yours, say you .... something new.
16 not mind / try

B **FIND THE GRAMMAR** Underline all the gerunds and infinitives in the "Answers" section on page 74.

PRONUNCIATION *Reduction of to in infinitives*

▶ 4:03 Notice how an unstressed **to** reduces to /tə/ in natural speech. Read and listen. Then listen again and repeat.

1 I decided to repaint the bedroom a happier color.

2 We plan to see the World Cup Finals.

3 She doesn't like to hear people talking on cell phones.

4 I know you'd like to choose a more cheerful color.

CONVERSATION MODEL

A ▶4:04 Read and listen to a conversation about likes and dislikes.

A: So tell me something about yourself.

B: What would you like to know?

A: Well, for example, what do you like doing in your free time?

B: Let's see. Most of all, I enjoy playing tennis. I think it's relaxing. What about you?

A: Well, I find tennis a little boring. But I <u>do</u> love going to the movies.

B: So do I. We should go to the movies together sometime, then.

B ▶4:05 **RHYTHM AND INTONATION** Listen again and repeat. Then practice the Conversation Model with a partner.

NOW YOU CAN Get to know a new friend

A **NOTEPADDING** List your likes and dislikes in gerund form.

Likes	Dislikes
cooking	skiing

Likes	Dislikes

 B **CONVERSATION ACTIVATOR** With a partner, personalize the Conversation Model, using your likes and dislikes in gerund form from your notepad. Change the time or occasion.

A: So tell me something about yourself.
B: What would you like to know?
A: Well, for example, what do you like doing .... ?
B: Let's see. Most of all, I enjoy .... I think it's .... What about you?
A: Well, ...
B: ....

DON'T STOP!
Ask about your partner's plans for this weekend or for a vacation. Use the following verbs and your own infinitives:
need   want
plan   would like
For example:
"What do you **plan to do** this weekend?"

Other times and occasions
• in your free time
• on weekends
• on vacations
• with your friends / family
• for lunch / dinner

RECYCLE THIS LANGUAGE.

Positive adjectives	Negative adjectives
awesome	boring
fantastic	awful
wonderful	horrible
great	terrible
terrific	disgusting
relaxing	frightening
interesting	scary
exciting	silly
thrilling	weird
fascinating	

C **CHANGE PARTNERS** Talk about other likes and dislikes.

GOAL Cheer someone up

CONVERSATION MODEL

A ▶4:06 Read and listen to someone trying to cheer a friend up.

A: You look down. What's up?

B: Oh, nothing serious. I'm just tired of the same old grind. But thanks for asking.

A: I know what you mean. I'm tired of working, too. How about going to a movie? That always helps me.

B: Great idea. Let's go this afternoon!

B ▶4:07 **RHYTHM AND INTONATION** Listen again and repeat. Then practice the Conversation Model with a partner.

▶4:08 **More adjectives**

down
sad
unhappy
upset
depressed

GRAMMAR *Gerunds as objects of prepositions*

A gerund can function as an object of a preposition.

	preposition	object
I'm afraid	of	flying.
She's bored	with	cooking.
She objects	to	discussing her feelings.

Be careful! Don't use an infinitive as the object of a preposition.

Don't say: Let's go to a movie instead of ~~to watch~~ TV.

GRAMMAR BOOSTER p. 136
• Negative gerunds

Expressions followed by gerunds

Adjective + preposition

angry about	afraid of
excited about	sick / tired of
depressed about	bored with
happy / sad about	crazy about

Verb + preposition

complain about	apologize for
talk about	believe in
worry about	object to
think about	

With How about or What about
How about [going to a movie]?
What about [leaving work early]?

A **GRAMMAR PRACTICE** Complete the descriptions with prepositions and gerunds.

Ted

Do you want to know what I think?

Ted is an extrovert. Like most extroverts, he's direct. And he's honest; he believes .... the truth to everyone.
1 tell

At his job, he works with other people and he never complains .... long hours. He works hard and doesn't worry .... work on weekends or holidays.
2 work
3 have to

He has a few fears, though. Most of all, he's afraid ....
4 fly

Nicole

Ted's wife, Nicole, on the other hand, is an introvert. But she doesn't object .... about herself from time to time.
5 talk

Right now, she's bored .... a student, and she's sick and tired
6 be

.... so many long reports and
7 write

.... exams every few weeks!
8 take

She's angry .... spend
9 have to

so much time in front of a computer.

However, unlike Ted, she's not at all afraid .... ! She's
10 fly

excited .... on
11 go

vacation.

B **PAIR WORK** Answer the questions about yourself, using gerunds. Then share the information with a partner.

Right now, what are you . . .	
happy about?	
exclted about?	
bored with?	
sick and tired of?	

> 66 Right now, I'm happy about getting engaged! 99

NOW YOU CAN Cheer someone up

A **NOTEPADDING** Make a list of things that you are tired of. Write them as gerunds.

What are you tired of?
studying so hard

B **CONVERSATION ACTIVATOR** With a partner, role-play cheering someone up. Use your notepad for ideas. Then change roles.

A: You look .... What's up?
B: Oh, nothing serious. I'm just tired of ....
   But thanks for asking.
A: I know what you mean. ....
B: ....

DON'T STOP!

Make more suggestions, using gerunds and infinitives.

RECYCLE THIS LANGUAGE.

Be sure [to get enough sleep].
You should think about [quitting your job].
What about [going out for a nice dinner]?
How about [getting a massage]?
If you [avoid drinking a lot of coffee],
   you [will sleep better].
That always helps me.
That's a good idea.
Don't expect [to feel better right away].

C **CHANGE PARTNERS** Cheer your new partner up.

GOAL Discuss personality and its origin

BEFORE YOU READ

EXPLORE YOUR IDEAS In what way does a parent's behavior affect a child's development?

READING ▶ 4:09

Personality: from Nature or Nurture?

What is personality? Many people define personality as a person's usual manner or style of behavior. These patterns of behavior tend to be predictable throughout a person's lifetime. Some people are introverts; others are extroverts. Some people have easygoing personalities: they are usually cheerful and calm and able to cope with life's difficulties without much trouble. Their emotions are usually under control: they don't get extremely angry about little things. Others, at the other end of the personality spectrum, are more emotional, experiencing higher highs and lower lows. Most people's personalities, however, don't fall at the extreme ends but rather fall somewhere in between.

Where do we get our personality? For hundreds of years, psychologists and ordinary people have never stopped debating this fascinating question. Some people think personality develops as a result of the environment—the combination of influences that we learn from, such as our families, our culture, our friends, and our education. The people who believe this theory believe that all babies are born without a personality and that it's the environment that determines, or forms, each child's personality. This school of thought is called the "nurture school."

At the other end of the continuum we find people who believe that personality is determined by "nature," or the characteristics we receive, or "inherit," from our parents biologically, through their genes. These people believe that our personality is not determined by the environment, but rather by genetics, and that each baby is born with a personality.

The "nature-nurture controversy" The nature-nurture controversy is very old. Experimental psychologists have tried to discover which of these two factors, genetics or the environment, is more important in forming our personality. However, it's very difficult, if not impossible, to conduct research on real people with real lives. There's just no way to put people in a laboratory and watch them develop. For this reason, there's no scientific way to settle the nature-nurture controversy. Recently, however, most researchers have come to believe that both the environment AND the genes—nurture and nature—work together and are both important.

Even though the experts have largely discarded the idea that personality development is so black and white, the nature-nurture controversy remains a popular discussion among friends. It seems that everyone has an opinion.

A **UNDERSTAND VOCABULARY FROM CONTEXT** Match the words and phrases in the two columns.

.... **1** genes

.... **2** environment

.... **3** emotions

.... **4** the "nature school" (of thought)

.... **5** the "nurture school" (of thought)

.... **6** personality

a a person's usual pattern of behavior

b what we feel, such as anger, love, and happiness

c the source of traits we inherit from our parents

d the world around us

e the belief that learning determines personality

f the belief that genetics determines personality

B **MAKE PERSONAL COMPARISONS** How is your personality similar to or different from those of your parents? If you have children, how are your children similar to or different from you? Use language from the Reading.

A **FRAME YOUR IDEAS** Complete the survey to find out if you are an introvert or an extrovert.

ARE YOU AN EXTROVERT OR AN INTROVERT?

Instructions: From each pair of personality traits, check one that sounds like <u>your</u> personality. At the end, add up your selections for each column. Then decide for yourself: Are you an introvert or an extrovert?

Extroverts tend to:	Introverts tend to:
1. ○ enjoy being in a group.	○ enjoy being alone.
2. ○ need to interact with others.	○ avoid interacting unnecessarily.
3. ○ be active.	○ be quiet.
4. ○ be interested in events.	○ be interested in feelings.
5. ○ talk without thinking.	○ think without talking.
6. ○ be easy to understand.	○ be hard to understand.
7. ○ know many people a little.	○ know few people, but well.
8. ○ talk.	○ listen.
9. ○ seek excitement.	○ seek peace.
10. ○ express their opinions openly.	○ keep their ideas to themselves.

Total extrovert selections [＿＿＿]   Total introvert selections [＿＿＿]

○ I'm an extrovert.   ○ I'm an introvert.   ○ I'm a mixture of both!

B **PAIR WORK** Discuss the personality traits you checked. For each, provide a real example from your life to explain your choices.

I'm pretty active. I like to go out almost every night, to the movies or to play sports.

I tend to stay home most nights. It gives me time to think.

C **DISCUSSION** Where do you think your personality came from, nurture or nature? Did your personality traits come from your parents' genes, or did you <u>learn</u> to be the way you are? Explain with examples using gerunds and infinitives.

RECYCLE THIS LANGUAGE.

[never] complain about ＿.	be crazy about ＿.
[sometimes] worry about ＿.	object to ＿.
[usually] apologize for ＿.	believe in ＿.
get [angry / excited / happy / sad] about ＿.	not care for ＿.
	prefer ＿.
be sick and tired of ＿.	avoid ＿.
be bored with ＿.	not mind ＿.
be afraid of ＿.	tend to ＿.

Text-mining (optional)
Find and underline three words or phrases in the Reading that were new to you. Use them in your Discussion.
For example: "easygoing."

BEFORE YOU LISTEN

EXPLORE YOUR IDEAS Do you think the first child in a family has different personality traits from those of siblings who are born later? Explain your answer.

LISTENING COMPREHENSION

A ▶4:10 **LISTEN FOR MAIN IDEAS** Read the statements. Then listen to all three parts of the discussion. Choose the statement that best expresses the main idea of the discussion.

☐ First-born children are often too critical of themselves.

☐ Children in the same family usually have personalities that are determined by order of birth.

☐ Children usually have personalities that are determined by genes.

B ▶4:11 **LISTEN FOR SPECIFIC INFORMATION** Read the exercise. Then listen to each part of the discussion again separately. Complete the exercise as you listen.

Part 1: Check <u>True</u> or <u>False</u> for each statement.

	True	False
1 Brian is usually dissatisfied with himself.	☐	☐
2 Brian obeys rules.	☐	☐
3 Brian does most things well.	☐	☐
4 Brian's mother thinks her husband pushed Brian to be successful.	☐	☐
5 Brian never liked being with adults when he was growing up.	☐	☐

Part 2: Complete each statement by circling the correct information.

1 Annie is (the middle child / the "baby").

2 Annie had (a lot of / only a little) time with her parents before her younger sister was born.

3 Annie is jealous of (Brian / Brian and Lucy).

4 Annie (breaks / obeys) rules.

5 Annie is (rebellious and / rebellious but not) popular.

Part 3: Circle the answer to each question.

1 How old was Annie when Lucy was born?
 a 13 years
 b 13 months

2 What does Lucy like most?
 a making other people laugh
 b laughing at other people

3 What did Lucy do to the dining room wall?
 a She painted it.
 b She washed it.

4 Why does Lucy drive her older siblings crazy?
 a She pays too much attention to them.
 b Others pay too much attention to her.

C **CLASSIFY INFORMATION** Check the most common birth position for each personality, according to the discussion. Listen again if necessary.

Personality traits	First child	Middle child	Youngest child
Breaks rules	☐	☐	☐
Feels less important than siblings	☐	☐	☐
Grows up fast	☐	☐	☐
Grows up slowly	☐	☐	☐
Has a lot of friends	☐	☐	☐
Is creative	☐	☐	☐
Is rebellious	☐	☐	☐
Is self-critical	☐	☐	☐
Plays by the rules	☐	☐	☐
Shows off	☐	☐	☐

NOW YOU CAN Examine the impact of birth order

A **FRAME YOUR IDEAS** Complete the checklist for yourself.

1 What's your birth position in your family?
- ○ I'm the first child or the only child in the family.
- ○ I'm a middle child—neither the first nor the last.
- ○ I'm the "baby"—the youngest child in the family.

2 What are your personality traits? (Check all that are true.)
- ○ I'm self-critical. I always feel I should do better.
- ○ I'm a rebel.
- ○ I'm popular. I have a lot of friends.
- ○ I feel less important than my older or younger siblings.
- ○ I love to clown around and make people laugh.
- ○ I can be lovable one minute and a rebel the next.
- ○ I'm creative.
- ○ I often feel jealous of my siblings.

B **GROUP WORK** Form three groups of students, according to your birth positions. Compare your checklists with other members of your group. Do you share the same personality traits? Report your findings to the class.

Group 1: first or only children
Group 2: middle children
Group 3: youngest children

> ❝ Almost everyone in our group checked 'I'm self-critical!' ❞

C **DISCUSSION** Talk about how birth order can affect the development of a person's personality.

Ideas
- genetics / nature
- the environment / nurture
- introverts and extroverts
- parents' behavior

REVIEW

A ▶4:12 Listen to the conversations. Then circle a word or phrase to complete each statement.

1 Andy is feeling (down / happy).

2 Mollie is (an extrovert / an introvert).

3 Greg is (an extrovert / an introvert).

4 Millie thinks (genetics / the environment) is the most important factor in personality development.

5 Vera thinks (genetics / the environment) is the most important factor in personality development.

B Complete the paragraph with the correct prepositions.

Extroverts don't worry .... talking in public. They believe .... being honest, and they get
                                         1   2
bored .... being alone. They may talk .... staying home and reading a book, but when they
         3   4
do, they complain .... having no one to talk to. They object .... being by themselves.
                      5   6

C Complete each personal statement with a gerund or infinitive phrase.

1 When I want to stay healthy, I avoid ....

2 I really enjoy .... on Saturdays and Sundays.

3 I wish other people would quit .... in the movies.

4 Two things I can't stand are .... and ....

5 On weekends, I dislike ....

6 If the weather is bad, I don't mind ....

7 Tomorrow I would really like ....

8 If I want to do well in this class, I need ....

9 Tomorrow I plan ....

10 I think most people are afraid of ....

11 I think people are usually excited about ....

12 Too many people complain about ....

13 My family worries most about ....

D Complete each statement. Circle the best answer.

1 John is such (an extrovert / an introvert). He doesn't like to talk about himself a lot.

2 Our usual pattern of behavior is our (personality / environment).

3 Another word for characteristics is (nurture / traits).

4 Many people believe that (self-criticism / birth order) affects personality development.

5 The nature-nurture controversy is an argument about the origin of the
   (environment / personality).

WRITING

Write at least two paragraphs about the personality of someone
you know well. Use vocabulary and ideas from Lessons 3 and 4.

For additional language practice . . .

♫ TOP NOTCH POP • Lyrics p. 154
"The Colors of Love"

[DIGITAL SONG] [DIGITAL KARAOKE]

WRITING BOOSTER p. 149
• Parallel structure
• Guidance for this writing exercise

ORAL REVIEW

PAIR WORK

1 Create a conversation for photo 1 in which the girl on the left cheers up her friend. Use gerunds and infinities.

2 Role-play a discussion between the two people in photo 2. They discuss the birth order of their siblings and their personalities.

GROUP WORK Choose one person to be the professor in photo 3. Help that person create a lecture about personality development. Then the other classmates listen to the lecture and ask questions.

You look down . . .

1

So, who is the youngest in your family?

2

Today we're discussing the nature-nurture controversy . . .

3

NOW I CAN

- ☐ Get to know a new friend.
- ☐ Cheer someone up.
- ☐ Discuss personality and its origin.
- ☐ Examine the impact of birth order.

PREVIEW

ART Exhibit

Drawing

Jewelry

Pottery

Fashion

Sculpture

BARKER STREET
GALLERY
OCT. 12–NOV. 24

Painting

Photography

 DIGITAL FLASH CARDS

A ▶ 4:15 **VOCABULARY • *Kinds of art*** Read and listen. Then listen again and repeat.

B **DISCUSSION** What kinds of art do you like? Which pieces of art in the Preview do you like? Why? Use some of the adjectives.

❝ I'm not really into paintings, but I think this one's beautiful. ❞

❝ I like jewelry, but I don't think the necklace is very interesting. ❞

Adjectives to describe art

beautiful	awful	feminine
exciting	boring	masculine
fascinating	weird	unusual
relaxing	silly	practical
thought-provoking	depressing	interesting

C ▶ 4:16 **PHOTO STORY** Read and listen to a conversation at an art show.

Lynn: Teo, this is just great. I had no idea you had so much talent!

Teo: Thank you!

Lynn: I mean it. Your work is very impressive.

Teo: It's so nice of you to say that. I don't think I'm particularly talented. I just love to paint.

Teo: Believe it or not, these were taken by Paul Johns.

Lynn: Your boss? How do you like that! They're really quite good.

Teo: I know. He doesn't look like the artistic type, does he?

Lynn: No. I had no idea he took photos. I guess you can't always judge a book by its cover.

Teo: Hey, this is an interesting piece. I kind of like it.

Lynn: You do? I find it a little weird, actually.

Teo: But that's what makes it so fascinating.

Lynn: Well, to each his own. I guess I'm just not really into abstract art.

D **ACTIVATE VOCABULARY** Circle the three kinds of art Lynn and Teo discuss:

painting	fashion	sculpture	photography	drawing	jewelry

E **FOCUS ON LANGUAGE** With a partner, discuss and find an underlined expression in the Photo Story to match each of the phrases.

1 I didn't know . . .

2 I don't really like . . .

3 Everyone has a different opinion.

4 I have some information that may surprise you.

5 I'm really surprised!

6 You can't really know someone just by looking at him or her.

7 In my opinion, it's . . .

SPEAKING

"" I prefer more realistic art. I'm just not into abstract paintings. ""

What kinds of art do you prefer? Explain why.

"" I'm into fashion. I like clothes that are really modern. ""

Art can be **realistic** . . .

or **abstract**.

It can be **traditional** . . .

or **modern**.

GOAL Recommend a museum

GRAMMAR *The passive voice*

Most sentences are in the active voice: the subject of a sentence performs the action of the verb. In the passive voice, the receiver of the action is the subject of the sentence.

Active voice: Architect Frank Gehry designed the Guggenheim Museum in Bilbao, Spain.

Passive voice: The Guggenheim Museum in Bilbao, Spain, was designed by architect Frank Gehry.

Form the passive voice with a form of <u>be</u> and the past participle of a verb.

These vases are made in Korea.
The museum was built in the 1990's.
The *Mona Lisa* has been shown at the Louvre Museum since 1797.

It is common to use the passive voice when the performer of the action is not known or not important. Use a <u>by</u> phrase in a passive voice sentence when it is important to identify the performer of an action.

Pottery is made by people in many parts of the world. (not important)
This bowl was found by someone in Costa Rica. (not important)
This dress was designed by Donatella Versace. (important)

> **GRAMMAR BOOSTER** p. 137
> • Transitive and intransitive verbs
> • The passive voice: other tenses

A UNDERSTAND THE GRAMMAR Read each passive voice sentence and decide if the <u>by</u> phrase is necessary. If it isn't necessary, cross it out.

1 The glass pyramids were added to the Louvre Museum in Paris by workers in 1989.

2 The sculpture *The Thinker* was created by French artist Auguste Rodin.

3 Antoni Gaudí designed and built some of the most famous buildings in Spain. His plans for the Casa Milà in Barcelona were completed by him in 1912.

4 The melody of "Ode to Joy" is known by people all over the world. It was written by German composer Ludwig van Beethoven.

5 China's famous Terracotta Army figures in Xi'an were discovered by farmers in 1974.

B GRAMMAR PRACTICE Change each sentence from the active to the passive voice. Use a <u>by</u> phrase.

1 Leonardo da Vinci painted the *Mona Lisa* in the sixteenth century.

....

2 Brazilian photographer Sebastião Salgado took that photograph in 2007.

....

3 Mexican filmmaker Alfonso Cuarón directed the 2013 3D film *Gravity*.

....

4 Japanese master printmaker Katsushika Hokusai made that print over a century ago.

....

5 Korean fashion designer Sang A Im-Propp created these beautiful handbags.

....

6 Weavers have produced beautiful Persian rugs for several thousand years.

....

CONVERSATION MODEL

A ▶ 4:17 Read and listen to someone recommend a museum.

A: Be sure not to miss the Louvre while you're in Paris.

B: Really? Why's that?

A: Well, for one thing, that famous painting, the *Mona Lisa*, is kept there.

B: No kidding! I've always wanted to see the *Mona Lisa*!

A: Well, they have a great collection of paintings. You'll love it.

B: Thanks for the suggestion!

The *Mona Lisa* by Leonardo Da Vinci

B ▶ 4:18 **RHYTHM AND INTONATION** Listen again and repeat. Then practice the Conversation Model with a partner.

PRONUNCIATION *Emphatic stress*

A ▶ 4:19 Notice how stress is emphasized to show enthusiasm. Read and listen. Then listen again and repeat.

1 No **KIDD**ing!　　**2** That's fan**TA**stic!　　**3** That's **PER**fect!　　**4** How **IN**teresting!

B Now practice saying the following statements with emphatic stress.

1 That's ter**RI**fic!　　**2** That's **WON**derful!　　**3** How ex**CI**ting!　　**4** How **NICE**!

THE GOLD MUSEUM - BOGOTÁ

Famous for its large collection of jewelry and sculpture

El Dorado's Raft (gold and emeralds)

NOW YOU CAN Recommend a museum

CONVERSATION ACTIVATOR With a partner, change the Conversation Model to recommend a museum. Use the information in the pictures or museums you know. Use the passive voice and emphatic stress. Then change roles.

A: Be sure not to miss .... while you're in ....
B: Really? Why's that?
A: Well, for one thing, ... is kept there.
B: .... ! I've always wanted to see ....
A: Well, they have a .... collection of .... You'll love it.
B: Thanks for the suggestion!

DON'T STOP!

- Recommend other things to see or do.

THE NATIONAL PALACE MUSEUM
TAIPEI

Known for its huge collection of traditional Chinese painting, pottery, and sculpture

The Chinese Cabbage sculpture (jade)

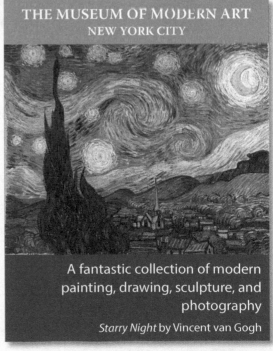

THE MUSEUM OF MODERN ART
NEW YORK CITY

A fantastic collection of modern painting, drawing, sculpture, and photography

Starry Night by Vincent van Gogh

GOAL Ask about and describe objects

CONVERSATION MODEL

A ▶4:20 Read and listen to someone asking about an object.

A: Excuse me. What's this figure made of?

B: Wood. It's handmade.

A: Really? Where was it made?

B: Mexico. What do you think of it?

A: It's fantastic!

B ▶4:21 **RHYTHM AND INTONATION** Listen again and repeat. Then practice the Conversation Model with a partner.

VOCABULARY *Objects, handicrafts, and materials*

A ▶4:22 Read and listen. Then listen again and repeat.

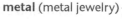

glass
(a glass pitcher)

silver
(a silver necklace)

gold
(a gold bracelet)

wood
(a wood figure)

cloth
(a cloth bag)

ceramic
(a ceramic plate)

stone
(a stone bowl)

B **PAIR WORK** Tell your partner about some of your favorite objects in your home.

> On my vacation last year, I bought a large stone bowl. It's in my kitchen, and I use it for serving.

GRAMMAR *The passive voice: questions*

Was this stone figure carved by hand?	Yes, it was. / No, it wasn't.
Were these wood bracelets made in Thailand?	Yes, they were. / No, they weren't.
What is this made of?	It's made of wood.
What is this ceramic bowl used for?	It's used for preparing food.
When was this picture painted?	It was painted in the 1980s.
Where were these cloth figures made?	In Brazil.
How were those handbags manufactured?	By machine.

GRAMMAR BOOSTER p. 138

- Yes / no questions in the passive voice: other tenses

A GRAMMAR PRACTICE Complete the questions in the interview. Use a question word and the passive voice.

> We interviewed Brian Tardiff at the Sanford Gallery about the exhibit of modern Hmong cloth quilts.
>
> **Q** ___Where are___ these quilts ___made___ ?
> _{1 make}
>
> **A** These beautiful quilts are made in Vietnam by women from the Hmong tribe.
>
> **Q** .... they .... of?
> _{2 make}
>
> **A** They're made of cloth. The pieces of cloth are cut by hand and sewn together.
>
> **Q** .... the cloth .... ?
> _{3 dye}
>
> **A** It's dyed in different colors, using plants and beeswax. It takes a lot of time.
>
> **Q** .... they .... ?
> _{4 sew}
>
> **A** They are sewn by hand. Each is unique.
>
> **Q** .... they .... for?
> _{5 use}
>
> **A** Many people just use them for decoration. However, Hmong culture doesn't have a written tradition, so some are used to tell stories about the women's lives.

B Complete the conversations. Write information questions, using the passive voice.

1 A: .... ?
   B: The glass cups? They were made by hand.

2 A: .... ?
   B: That silver bowl? It's used for serving sugar.

3 A: .... ?
   B: This beautiful figure? It's made of gold.

4 A: .... ?
   B: These wood chairs? They were made in Venezuela.

5 A: .... ?
   B: That Chinese bag? It was made by machine.

6 A: .... ?
   B: This cup? It's made of ceramic.

NOW YOU CAN Ask about and describe objects

A CONVERSATION ACTIVATOR With a partner, change the Conversation Model to ask about and describe one of the objects. Use the Vocabulary. Then change roles.

A: Excuse me. What .... made of?
B: ....
A: .... Where .... made?
B: .... What do you think of .... ?
A: ....

DON'T STOP!
- Ask about other objects.
- Ask other passive voice questions.

a figure / Greece

a plate / Italy

dolls / Russia

cups / Thailand

a vase / China

B CHANGE PARTNERS Practice the conversation again about other objects.

C DISCUSSION Describe an object in your own home. Ask your classmates questions about the objects they describe.

" In my living room, I have a small figure. It's made of wood. It's a piece of traditional art. I bought it on my vacation last year. "

RECYCLE THIS LANGUAGE.

fantastic	cool
awesome	interesting
terrific	beautiful

GOAL Talk about artistic talent

BEFORE YOU READ

WARM-UP Do you do anything artistic? Do you paint, draw, or do handicrafts? Why or why not?

> 66 I paint sometimes.
> I find it relaxing. 99

> 66 Actually, I'm not interested in art.
> I don't really think I have any ability. 99

READING ▶ 4:23

Is it talent or hard work?

All young children scribble, doodle, and draw stick figures.

When children are asked to draw or paint a picture, they are happy to oblige. And they are willing to talk about and show their creation to anyone they meet. But when adults are asked to do the same thing, they typically get nervous and refuse to even try, claiming that they have no talent.

Most adults see themselves as lacking the "artistic gene." However, when you look at drawings made by artists when they were children, their work doesn't differ much from the scribbles and stick figures all children draw when they are young. When Don Lipski, who makes a successful living as a professional artist, looks back at drawings that he made as a child, he doesn't find any early evidence of his own artistic talent. "I was always making things . . . doodling and putting things together. I didn't think of myself as a creative person. I was just doing what all kids do."

The general belief is that artistic talent is something one is born with: a person either has talent or does not. Clearly, great artists like Michelangelo or Picasso had natural talent and possessed more artistic ability than the average person. However, one factor that isn't often considered is the role that years of training, practice, and hard work have played in the creation of great pieces of art. In addition, most artists are successful because they are passionate about their art—they love what they do. Their passion motivates them to continue to create—and improve their ability—day after day. While natural talent may be an advantage, hard work appears to be a necessary part of the creative process.

In *Drawing on the Right Side of the Brain*, author Betty Edwards argues that while few people are born with natural artistic talent, all of us have the potential to improve our artistic ability. We just have to be willing to keep working at it. She claims that anyone can learn to use the right side of the brain, the side that governs visual skills like drawing and painting. In other words, artistic ability can be learned.

A **RECOGNIZE THE MAIN IDEA** Choose the main idea of the article.

  a Artistic skill can be taught.

  b Children are better artists than adults.

  c To draw well, you have to be born with artistic talent.

  d Few people are born with artistic talent.

B **IDENTIFY SUPPORTING DETAILS** Read each statement. Check <u>True</u> or <u>False</u>, according to the article. Support your choice with details from the article.

		True	False
1	Young children generally don't worry if they are talented or not.	☐	☐
2	Most adults think they are not talented.	☐	☐
3	It's easy to see which children are going to be artists when you look at their drawings.	☐	☐
4	There isn't much difference between famous artists and other people.	☐	☐
5	Talent is all one needs to create great artistic work.	☐	☐
6	People who don't have natural talent can improve their artistic skill.	☐	☐

C **PARAPHRASE** Read the paragraph in the article about *Drawing on the Right Side of the Brain* again. In your own words, restate Betty Edwards's theory about artistic ability.

> According to Betty Edwards, . . .

DIGITAL
MORE
RCISES

NOW YOU CAN Talk about artistic talent

A **FRAME YOUR IDEAS** Complete the survey. Then compare responses with a partner.

Who's Got Talent?

1. Do any of your family members or friends have artistic talent? ○ yes ○ no

   Relationship to you: _____

   In which of the arts? _____

   Where do you think this talent comes from?

   _____

2. Do you think you have natural artistic talent?
   ○ yes ○ no ○ not sure

3. Do other people think you're talented?
   ○ yes ○ no ○ not sure

4. How would you rate your own artistic talent on a scale of 1 to 5?

1	2	3	4	5
POOR		AVERAGE		EXCELLENT

5. In which of the arts do you think you may have talent? Explain.

   example
   ☑ music <u>I sing and play several musical instruments</u>.

   ○ music _____

   ○ drawing / painting _____

   ○ handicrafts _____

   ○ acting _____

   ○ dancing _____

   ○ photography _____

   ○ other _____

B **DISCUSSION** Do you think people are born with artistic talent? Or is it developed through years of training, practice, and hard work?

Text-mining (optional)
Find and underline three words or phrases in the Reading that were new to you. Use them in your Discussion.
For example: "have talent."

BEFORE YOU LISTEN

DIGITAL
FLASH
CARDS
A ▶ 4:24 **VOCABULARY** • *Passive participial phrases* Read and listen.
Then listen again and repeat.

Vincent van Gogh
painter

be inspired by He is inspired by nature. He tries to capture nature's beauty in his photographs.

be influenced by She was influenced by Stella McCartney's work. You can see similarities between McCartney's fashion designs and her own.

Stella McCartney
fashion designer

be fascinated by He has always been fascinated by the life of Vincent van Gogh. He thinks the artist was extremely fascinating.

be moved by You will be moved by Charlie Chaplin's films. Even though they are funny, their themes of life and love really touch your heart.

Charles Chaplin
actor, filmmaker

B **PAIR WORK** Tell your partner what inspires, influences, interests, fascinates, and moves you. Use passive participial phrases.

❝ I'm inspired by my parents. They work really hard. ❞

LISTENING COMPREHENSION

A ▶ 4:25 **UNDERSTAND FROM CONTEXT** Listen to the interviews. Complete each statement with the name of the artist.

1 Burt Hildegard is fascinated by the work of ....
2 Susan Wallach is influenced by the work of ....
3 Katherine Wolf is inspired by the work of ....
4 Nick Jenkins is moved by the work of ....

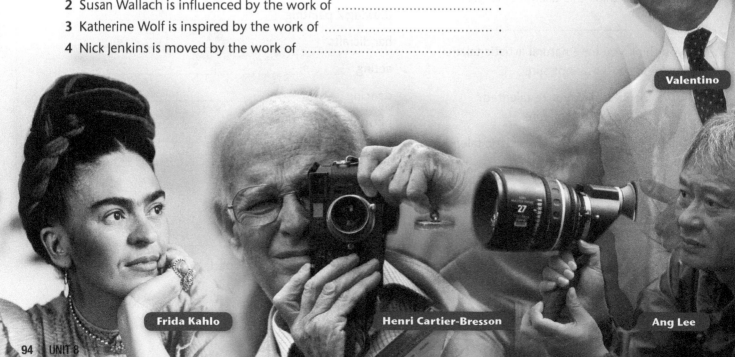

Valentino

Frida Kahlo

Henri Cartier-Bresson

Ang Lee

B   ▶4:26 **LISTEN TO TAKE NOTES**   Listen again to each interview and write some of
the details you hear about each artist. Compare notes with a partner.

1 Ang Lee	2 Henri Cartier-Bresson	3 Valentino	4 Frida Kahlo
explores culture	took black-and-white photos	is Italian	was sick as a child

C   **DISCUSSION**   Which of the artists described in the Listening do you find the most
fascinating? Use your notes to explain why.

NOW YOU CAN   Discuss your favorite artists

A   **FRAME YOUR IDEAS**   Complete the questionnaire. Then compare answers with a partner.

WHICH QUALITIES ATTRACT YOU TO AN ARTIST?
Check all that apply.

HIS OR HER WORK . . .
- ○ is realistic / traditional.
- ○ is abstract / modern.
- ○ is easy to understand.
- ○ makes you think.
- ○ touches your heart.
- ○ makes you laugh.
- ○ other: _____

HE OR SHE . . .
- ○ is a rebel.
- ○ is creative.
- ○ tries new things.
- ○ has his or her own style.
- ○ inspires people.
- ○ other: _____

Types of artists
a painter
a writer
a sculptor
a filmmaker / director
a fashion designer
an architect
a photographer
an actor
a singer
a dancer

Types of art
drawing
painting
sculpture
photography
jewelry
pottery
fashion
handicrafts

B   **NOTEPADDING**   On your notepad, write about some of your favorite artists.

	Artist's name	Type of artist	Why I like this artist
1			
2			
3			

C   **GROUP WORK**   Discuss your favorite artists. Tell your class why you like them.
Ask your classmates questions about the artists they describe.

I'm a real fan of the Mexican painters Frida Kahlo and Diego Rivera. I'm fascinated by their lives.

Donatella Versace is my favorite designer. Her fashions are so creative!

One of my favorite Japanese artists is Naoki Urasawa. His drawings in the comic book *Yawara!* are really exciting.

REVIEW

A ▶ 4:27 Listen and write the letter of the piece of art each person is talking about. Then listen again and circle the best way to complete each statement.

a 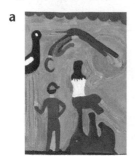 b  c  d  e

.... **1** She thinks it's (beautiful / ugly / abstract).

.... **2** He thinks it's (traditional / ugly / fascinating). She thinks it's (fantastic / OK / abstract).

.... **3** She thinks it's (OK / awful / great). He thinks it's too (abstract / dark / traditional).

B On a separate sheet of paper, change each sentence from active to passive voice.

1 César Pelli designed the Petronas Twin Towers in Kuala Lumpur.

2 The great Iranian filmmaker Majid Majidi directed *Children of Heaven* in 1998.

3 Henri Matisse made the print *Icarus* in 1947.

4 Annie Leibovitz took that photograph of John Lennon in 1980.

5 The Japanese artist Hokusai produced *The Great Wave of Kanagawa* in the early 1830s.

C List materials under each category. Answers may vary.

Materials that are expensive	Materials that weigh a lot	Materials that break easily
gold		

D Complete the statements.

1 The art of designing clothes is called ....

2 One type of .... is a figure carved from wood or stone.

3 Two types of metal often used to make jewelry are .... and ....

4 Art in a conservative style from the past is called .... art.

5 A piece of art made with a pen or pencil is called a ....

For additional language practice . . .

♫ TOP NOTCH POP • Lyrics p. 154
"To Each His Own"

DIGITAL SONG | DIGITAL KARAOKE

WRITING

Choose a favorite object that decorates your home. Describe it in a paragraph.

WRITING BOOSTER p. 150
• Providing supporting details
• Guidance for this writing exercise

Ideas
• a painting or drawing
• a photo or poster
• a piece of furniture
• a figure or sculpture
• a plate, bowl, or vase
• (your own idea) __

ORAL REVIEW

CONTEST Look at the page for one minute and close your books. Using the passive voice, who can describe the most objects and art?

The horse figure is made of __. The statue of David is kept in the __.

1

PAIR WORK

1 Create a conversation for the man and woman. Recommend a museum. Start like this:

Be sure not to miss the __ while you're in __.

2 Create a conversation for the customer and the store clerk. Ask about the objects. Start like this:

Excuse me. What's this __ made of?

DISCUSSION Talk about the pieces of art in the photos. Say what you like or don't like about each one.

2

THE GREAT MUSEUMS OF EUROPE

The Accademia Gallery
FLORENCE, ITALY

The world's largest collection of statues by Michelangelo!

David by Michelangelo

Musée d'Orsay
PARIS, FRANCE

Home of the best collection of 19th-century French art, including famous painters such as Monet, Degas, and Renoir

Apples and Oranges by Paul Cézanne

China

India

Peru

Sweden

✓ **NOW I CAN**

☐ Recommend a museum.
☐ Ask about and describe objects.
☐ Talk about artistic talent.
☐ Discuss my favorite artists.

Living in Cyberspace

COMMUNICATION GOALS
1 Troubleshoot a problem.
2 Compare product features.
3 Describe how you use the Internet.
4 Discuss the impact of the Internet.

PREVIEW

x

Our Community

Friends | Search | Home

FRANK CARUSO

✎ Edit

🔍 Search

✍ Messages

📷 My photo albums

🎥 Videos

👥 Groups

⬆ Upload

 Frank Caruso Hey, I'm in Rome now! How do you like my new profile pic? That's the Colosseum behind me. This place is awesome!

 Kathy Chu Wow! You take good selfies, Frank! You look like you're having fun! Hey, didn't you just post a message from Tokyo two days ago?

 Frank Caruso I did. But I've always wanted to see Italy, so someone suggested visiting my airline's web page to look for specials. I got a great deal on a return ticket with a stop here. I'm heading back home to Boston on Friday. Did you all catch the Japan photos I posted?

 Nardo Madureira No. What album are they in?

 Frank Caruso Actually, they're not here. They're on that new photo-sharing site, GlobalPhoto. Log on and add me to your friends. Or I can send you a link. Click on it to go right to the pics.

 Kathy Chu Well, I just looked and they're very cool. Can't wait to see the ones from Italy. I hope they're as nice as the ones from Japan! Nice chatting with you guys! Ciao!

A **PAIR WORK** Read the posts on the social network website. Are you on any similar sites? Do you post regularly? Why or why not?

B **DISCUSSION** Discuss these questions.

1 What photo-sharing services do you know about online? Do you store your photos on any of these sites? What are the advantages and disadvantages of photo-sharing services?

2 Have you ever posted photos while you were traveling? Do you know anyone who has?

C ▶5:02 **PHOTO STORY** Read and listen to a conversation in an office.

  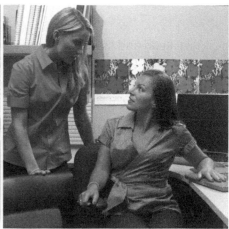

Amy: What are you doing here at this hour? I wasn't sure I'd find you.

Dee: Oh hi, Amy. I'm just fooling around online. I guess I forgot about the time!

Amy: Am I interrupting you?

Dee: Not at all. Paul and I are just instant messaging.

Amy: Sorry to bother you. But I'm a little worried about something.

Dee: What's wrong?

Amy: I just got this e-mail from someone I don't know, and I clicked on the attachment to see what it was. My computer totally crashed. Everything froze, and no matter what I do, nothing happens.

Dee: Actually, you should never open an attachment if you don't know the sender. It could be malware or carry a virus.

Amy: I know. I don't know what I was thinking! It just happened so fast.

Dee: Look. First, try shutting down and restarting, OK? Sometimes that takes care of it.

Amy: You think that would work?

Dee: It couldn't hurt. Listen, Paul's still there. Let me send a quick response, OK? I'll just be a second.

Amy: No problem. I'll go and try restarting to see if that does the trick.

D **FOCUS ON LANGUAGE** Look at the five expressions from the Photo Story. Write the letter of the meaning of each expression. (Two expressions have the same meaning.)

.... **1** just fooling around

.... **2** takes care of it

.... **3** couldn't hurt

.... **4** I'll just be a second

.... **5** does the trick

a won't take a long time

b not doing anything serious

c is worth trying

d fixes the problem

SPEAKING

Do you know how to solve computer problems? Complete the chart. Then compare answers with a partner and discuss some possible solutions.

Do you know what to do if . . .	Yes	No	Not sure
1 you think you have a virus?	☐	☐	☐
2 your printer won't print?	☐	☐	☐
3 you click on a link and nothing happens?	☐	☐	☐
4 your computer is really slow?	☐	☐	☐
5 your computer crashes?	☐	☐	☐
6 you forget your password?	☐	☐	☐

Some computer solutions
- try restarting
- check if it's turned on
- buy a new computer
- [your own idea]

GOAL Troubleshoot a problem

CONVERSATION MODEL

A ▶5:03 Read and listen to people troubleshooting a computer problem.

A: Eugene, could you take a look at this?

B: Sure. What's the problem?

A: Well, I clicked on the toolbar to save a file, and the computer crashed.

B: Why don't you try restarting? That sometimes works.

A: OK. I'll give that a try.

B ▶5:04 **RHYTHM AND INTONATION** Listen again and repeat. Then practice the Conversation Model with a partner.

▶5:05 **Ways to reassure someone**
That sometimes works.
That sometimes helps.
That sometimes does the trick.

DIGITAL FLASH CARDS

VOCABULARY *The computer screen, components, and commands*

A ▶5:06 Read and listen. Then listen again and repeat.

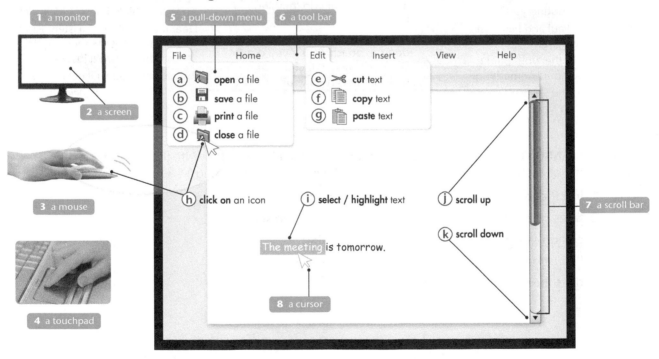

1 a monitor
2 a screen
3 a mouse
4 a touchpad
5 a pull-down menu
6 a tool bar
7 a scroll bar
8 a cursor

File   Home   Edit   Insert   View   Help

(a) open a file
(b) save a file
(c) print a file
(d) close a file
(e) cut text
(f) copy text
(g) paste text
(h) click on an icon
(i) select / highlight text
(j) scroll up
(k) scroll down

The meeting is tomorrow.

B ▶5:07 **LISTEN TO ACTIVATE VOCABULARY** Listen. Check the computer command each person needs.

1 He needs to click on . . .	☐	☐	☐	☐	☐	☐	☐	☐
2 She needs to click on . . .	☐	☐	☐	☐	☐	☐	☐	☐
3 He needs to click on . . .	☐	☐	☐	☐	☐	☐	☐	☐
4 She needs to click on . . .	☐	☐	☐	☐	☐	☐	☐	☐
5 He needs to click on . . .	☐	☐	☐	☐	☐	☐	☐	☐
6 She needs to click on . . .	☐	☐	☐	☐	☐	☐	☐	☐

GRAMMAR *The infinitive of purpose*

GRAMMAR BOOSTER p. 139
- Expressing purpose with <u>in order to</u> and <u>for</u>

An infinitive can be used to express a purpose.

I scrolled down to read the text. (= because I wanted to read the text)
Put the cursor on the toolbar to choose a file. (= if you want to choose a file)

Answering a <u>Why</u> question with an infinitive of purpose is similar to answering with <u>Because</u>.

Why did you click on that icon?   To save the file before I close it. (= Because I want to save it.)
Why did you highlight that word?   To select it so I can copy it. (= Because I want to copy it.)

A **FIND THE GRAMMAR** Look at the Conversation Model on page 100. Find an infinitive of purpose. Restate the sentence, using <u>because</u>.

B **PAIR WORK** Look at Cathy's to-do list. Ask and answer questions, using infinitives of purpose.

    ❝ Why is Cathy going shopping? ❞

             ❝ To get something for dinner. ❞

TO DO TODAY
- go shopping – get something for dinner
- call Dad – wish him Happy Birthday!
- meet Brandy – talk about next weekend
- talk to Mark – ask for help with scanner
- e-mail Hillary – send her my new photos
- drop off car at service station – fix windshield wipers
- visit Katonah Museum – see new art exhibit
- call salon – make appointment for manicure

C **GRAMMAR PRACTICE** Complete each sentence in your own way. Use infinitives of purpose.

1 Don't forget to click on the save icon *to save your document* .

2 You can click on the print icon ....

3 Put the cursor on the pull-down menu ....

4 I bought a new scanner ....

5 I e-mailed my friend ....

6 I connected to the Internet ....

NOW YOU CAN Troubleshoot a problem

A **CONVERSATION ACTIVATOR** With a partner, change the Conversation Model. Create a conversation in which one of you asks for help with a computer problem. Use the computer vocabulary from page 100 and an infinitive of purpose. Then change roles.

A: .... , could you take a look at this?
B: Sure. .... ?
A: Well, I clicked on .... to .... , and ....
B: Why don't you try .... ? That ....
A: .... I'll give that a try.

 DON'T STOP!
- Discuss other problems.
- Offer other suggestions.

RECYCLE THIS LANGUAGE.
- The computer crashes.
- The screen freezes.
- The printer won't print.
- The file won't [open / close / print].
- The [mouse] doesn't work.
- Nothing happens.
- (your own idea) ___

B **CHANGE PARTNERS** Practice the conversation again with other problems.

GOAL Compare product features

GRAMMAR *Comparisons with* <u>as</u> . . . <u>as</u>

GRAMMAR BOOSTER p. 139
- <u>As</u> . . . <u>as</u> to compare adverbs
- Comparatives and superlatives: review
- Comparison with adverbs

To express similarity

Use <u>as</u> . . . <u>as</u> with an adjective to indicate how two things are equal or the same. Use the adverb <u>just</u> for emphasis.

> The new speakers are as good as the old ones.
> The iFriend tablet is just as nice as the F40.

Use the adverb <u>almost</u> in affirmative statements to indicate that two things are very similar but not exactly the same.

> The Zeta B is almost as fast as the Panasox.

To express difference

Use <u>not as</u> . . . <u>as</u> to indicate how two things are different. Use <u>not quite</u> when the difference is very small. Use <u>not nearly</u> to indicate that there's a big difference.

> Our new printer isn't as noisy as the old one.
> The G4 isn't quite as expensive as the Z90.
> The Panasox isn't nearly as affordable as the Zeta B.

You can use shortened statements with <u>as</u> when the meaning is clear.

> The old monitor was great. But the new one is just as good. (= just as good as the old one)
> Have you seen Carl's new laptop? My laptop isn't as nice. (= as nice as his laptop)

A GRAMMAR PRACTICE Read each statement about a product. Write a sentence with <u>as</u> . . . <u>as</u> and the cue to compare the products.

1 The new Shine keyboard is popular. The one from Digitek is popular, too.

(just) ....

2 The XCue joystick is easy to use. The JRock joystick is also easy to use.

(just) ....

3 The C50 monitor is large. The C30 monitor is a little larger than the C50.

(almost) ....

4 Comtec's new mini-tablet is very small. Sango's new mini-tablet is also very small.

(just) ....

5 The CCV speakers are very powerful. The Soundtec speakers are much more powerful.

(not / nearly) ....

6 The Icon monitors are very inexpensive. The Sentinel monitors are a little more expensive.

(not / quite) ....

a joystick

B On a separate sheet of paper, write five statements comparing things you are familiar with. Use <u>as</u> . . . <u>as</u>.

> In my opinion, the Mardino sports car isn't nearly as good as the Strega.

Ideas for comparisons
- cars
- electronic products
- stores
- restaurants
- (your own idea) ___

PRONUNCIATION *Stress in* <u>as</u> . . . <u>as</u> *phrases*

A ▶5:08 Read and listen. Then listen again and repeat.

1 The new printer is as slow as the old one.

2 My old smart phone is just as small as the new one.

3 The X12 mouse isn't nearly as nice as the X30.

4 The M200 keyboard isn't quite as cheap as the Z6.

B Read the statements you wrote in Exercise B on page 102 aloud, paying attention to stress.

CONVERSATION MODEL

A ▶5:09 Listen to someone compare product features.

A: I'm thinking about getting a new game controller.

B: Oh, yeah? What kind?

A: Everyone says I should get a Macro.

B: Well, I've heard that the Panatel is as good as the Macro, but it costs a lot less.

A: Really? I'll check it out.

B ▶5:10 **RHYTHM AND INTONATION** Listen again and repeat. Then practice the Conversation Model with a partner.

NOW YOU CAN Compare product features

A **CONVERSATION ACTIVATOR** With a partner, change the Conversation Model, using the magazine ratings to compare features of different products. Use <u>as</u> . . . <u>as</u>. Then change roles.

A: I'm thinking about getting a new ....

B: .... ? What kind?

A: Everyone says I should get ....

B: Well, I've heard that ....

A: Really? ....

DON'T STOP!
• Ask about other features.

RECYCLE THIS LANGUAGE.

Which . . .
is more popular?	is newer?
is easier / harder to use?	is quieter / noisier?
is lighter / heavier?	is slower / faster?
is larger / smaller?	has more features?
is less / more expensive?	looks nicer?
costs less / more?	gets better reviews?

B **CHANGE PARTNERS** Now practice the conversation again, using other products and features.

Buyer's Friend *Magazine*

Our recommendations!

■ eMax Wireless Mouse	very good	US $25
■ eMax X15 Wireless Keyboard	very comfortable	US $30
■ eMax Y80 Webcam	easy to use	US $52
■ eMax Z40 Monitor	15 inches / 38 centimeters	US $250

THE ELECTRONICS GUIDE

YOUR BEST BUYS!

Klick Wireless Mouse	very good	US $12
Klick P40 Wireless Keyboard	very comfortable	US $25
Klick Ultra Webcam	easy to use	US $52
Klick P20 Monitor	19 inches / 48.3 centimeters	US $99

GOAL Describe how you use the Internet

BEFORE YOU LISTEN

DIGITAL FLASH CARDS

▶5:11 **VOCABULARY** • *Internet activities* Read and listen. Then listen again and repeat.

visit a website   go to a specific address on the Internet and read its content

surf the Internet   visit a lot of different websites for information that interests you

join (an online group)   become a member of an Internet group to meet friends and share information about your hobbies and interests

post (a message)   add your comments to an online discussion on a message board, a blog, or a social networking site

attach (a file)   place a document or photo into an e-mail

upload (a file)   move a document, music file, or picture from a personal computer, phone, or MP3 player onto the Internet

share (a link)   send an e-mail or post a message with the address of an interesting website you want someone to visit

download an application   download a useful program that you can use to play games, get information, or perform tasks

send an instant message   "chat" with someone online in real time by typing messages

look up information   go to a website to learn about something

Remember also:
- download (a file)
- stream a video
- check e-mail

LISTENING COMPREHENSION

A ▶5:12 **LISTEN FOR THE MAIN IDEA** Listen to people describe how they use the Internet. Write a checkmark next to the person who seems to enjoy the Internet the least. Explain your answer.

☐ **1** George Thomas   ☐ **2** Sonia Castro   ☐ **3** Robert Kuan   ☐ **4** Nadia Montasser

B ▶5:13 **LISTEN FOR DETAILS** Listen again and check the activities each person does.

	George Thomas	Sonia Castro	Robert Kuan	Nadia Montasser
buys products	☐	☐	☐	☐
downloads music	☐	☐	☐	☐
checks the latest news	☐	☐	☐	☐
participates in online groups	☐	☐	☐	☐
plays online games	☐	☐	☐	☐
sends instant messages	☐	☐	☐	☐
surfs the Internet	☐	☐	☐	☐
uploads photos	☐	☐	☐	☐
uses a computer at work	☐	☐	☐	☐

A   **FRAME YOUR IDEAS** Complete the survey about your own Internet use.

New Tab   ×

Internet User Survey

1. **I usually spend ___ hours a week online.**
    ○ 0 – 10   ○ 11 – 20   ○ 21 – 30   ○ 31 – 40   ○ 41 – 50   ○ over 50

2. **I use . . .**
    ○ a desktop   ○ a laptop   ○ a smart phone   ○ a tablet   ○ (none of these)

3. **I use the Internet . . .**
    ○ for work   ○ for study   ○ for fun   ○ I never use the Internet.

4. **I use the Internet . . .**

    ○ to search for new websites   ○ to send instant messages   ○ to download music
    ○ to upload photos   ○ to keep in touch with friends ○ to upload videos
    ○ to download photos   ○ to keep in touch with family ○ to download videos
    ○ to design websites   ○ to meet new people   ○ to send and receive e-mail
    ○ to look up information   ○ to watch movies   ○ to play games
    ○ to create art   ○ to look at my bank accounts   ○ to pay bills
    ○ to shop for things   ○ to sell things   ○ to read or watch the news
    ○ to take classes   ○ to practice English   ○ to just fool around
                                                                  ○ other: ....

5. **Check the statements that are true about you.**
    ○ People consider me to be a technology expert. They come to me for help.
    ○ You could say I'm an Internet addict. I'm always online.
    ○ Compared to most people, I spend a lot of time on the Internet.
    ○ I spend just as much time on the Internet as most people.
    ○ I don't spend nearly as much time on the Internet as most people.
    ○ I'm really not comfortable using the Internet.

B   **GROUP WORK** Walk around your classroom and ask your
classmates about their Internet use. Ask questions
to get more information and take notes.

Ideas for questions
Why . . . ?   When . . . ?
Where . . . ?   How . . . ?

Find someone who. . .	Name	Notes
is an Internet expert.		
is an Internet addict.		
isn't comfortable using the Internet.		
uses the Internet to meet people.		
uses the Internet to avoid people.		

C   **DISCUSSION** Tell your class what you
found out about your classmates and
how they use the Internet.

❝ May spends a lot of time online. She uses her
tablet to meet new people and keep in touch
with friends. Gary spends a lot of time online
with his smart phone. He uploads photos and . . . ❞

GOAL Discuss the impact of the Internet

BEFORE YOU READ

1 What kinds of problems have you had on the Internet?

2 What kinds of Internet problems have you heard about on the news?

READING ▶ 5:14

Identity Thieves Steal 40 Million Credit Card Numbers

Eleven hackers around the world were accused of stealing more than 40 million credit card numbers on the Internet. They included three people from the U.S. who are accused of hacking into the wireless networks of popular online stores.

Once inside these networks, they searched for customers' credit card numbers, passwords, and personal information so they could pretend to be those customers. When the identity theft was completed, credit card numbers and other details were then sold on the Internet, allowing criminals to withdraw thousands of dollars at a time from ATMs.

Computer Viruses Are Getting Harder to Prevent

"We're losing the battle against computer viruses," says David Farber, professor of computer science at Carnegie Mellon University. These viruses, which can enter computer systems through junk e-mail from hackers, have reached epidemic proportions, slowing down computers— and sometimes causing whole office computer systems to crash—in both large and small companies. In one year alone, they were reported to have caused $13 billion USD in damage.

Companies have been trying for years to protect themselves with anti-virus programs, but criminals are creating newer, improved viruses faster than these programs can keep up with.

Cyberbullying Leads to Teenager's Death

Megan Taylor Meier, age 13, joined an online social networking group where she became online friends with a 16-year-old boy named Josh. Megan and Josh never communicated by phone or in person, but she enjoyed exchanging messages with him in the group.

Over time, Josh changed. He began to bully her daily—criticizing her personality and telling her what a bad person she was. Some of their communications were posted so everyone could see them. Josh's last message to her said, "The world would be a better place without you." A short time later, Megan committed suicide.

After her death, it was discovered that there was no "Josh." The messages came from the mother of one of Megan's classmates. The mother had been angry with Megan because she believed Megan had said some untrue things about her daughter.

A UNDERSTAND FROM CONTEXT Use the context of the articles to help you to complete each definition.

.... 1 A hacker is . . .

.... 2 A computer virus is . . .

.... 3 A criminal is . . .

.... 4 Junk e-mail is . . .

.... 5 An anti-virus program is . . .

.... 6 A cyberbully is . . .

.... 7 An identity thief is . . .

a a software program that causes problems in computers.

b a software program that tries to stop the spread of viruses.

c a person who enters computer systems without permission.

d a person who steals other people's personal information.

e an advertisement you didn't request.

f a person who breaks the law; for example, by stealing money.

g a person who sends cruel and negative messages to another person online.

DIGITAL
MORE
EXERCISES

B RELATE TO PERSONAL EXPERIENCE What news stories have you heard about the Internet? Do you ever worry about using the Internet? Why or why not?

A   **NOTEPADDING**   With a partner, discuss each statement. Write at least one good change and one bad change for each.

1 | The Internet has changed the way people find information.

Good changes:

Bad changes:

2 | The Internet has changed the way people work in offices.

Good changes:

Bad changes:

3 | The Internet has changed the way people shop.

Good changes:

Bad changes:

4 | The Internet has changed the way people communicate.

Good changes:

Bad changes:

B   **DISCUSSION**   Do you think that computers and the Internet have brought more benefits or more problems? Support your opinions with examples.

Text-mining (optional)
Find and underline three words or phrases in the Reading that were new to you. Use them in your Discussion.
For example: "exchanging messages."

In my opinion, there are more benefits than problems. For example, it's easy to look up information, and it's really fast.

I think the Internet is OK, but there are really too many problems. First of all, you have to be very careful if you shop online with a credit card.

REVIEW

A ► 5:15 Listen to the conversations. Circle T for true and F for false. Then listen again and infer how to complete each statement.

1	She recommends the C40.	T	F
2	She recommends the Hip web camera.	T	F
3	He recommends the new Sender tablet.	T	F
4	He recommends the Play Zone 3.	T	F

1 The C40's monitor is .... the X8's.
   a the same size as   **b** larger than   **c** smaller than

2 The Hip web camera is .... the Pentac web camera.
   a the same price as   **b** cheaper than   **c** more expensive than

3 Sender's new model is .... Sender's old model.
   a the same as   **b** nicer than   **c** worse than

4 Play Zone 3 is .... Play Zone 2.
   a as cool as   **b** less cool than   **c** more cool than

B Answer each question in your own words, using infinitives of purpose.

1 Why do people join social networking sites? ....

2 Why do people send instant messages? ....

3 Why do people surf the Internet? ....

4 Why do people shop online? ....

5 Why are you studying English? ....

C Complete each statement.

1 .... on an icon on the screen to select it.

2 If you want to print a document, click on the print icon on the ....

3 To read more text on your monitor's .... , use the scroll .... to scroll down.

4 Click on <u>File</u> on the toolbar so you can choose an icon from the .... menu.

5 When you're finished working on a document, don't forget to .... it before you close the file.

D Unscramble the letters of the words in the box to complete each sentence.

chatated	clorls	doalwond	esmou	rekcha	rusvi

1 Last year, a .... got into the company's computer systems and stole important information.

2 Use the .... to click on a file and open it.

3 It isn't difficult to .... songs from the Internet.

4 Use the .... bar to see more text on the screen.

5 Her computer isn't working now because she downloaded a .... from a piece of junk e-mail.

6 I .... the photos to the e-mail I sent this morning.

WRITING

Write two paragraphs about the benefits and the problems of the Internet. Use your notepads from page 107 for support.

For additional language practice . . .

♫ TOP NOTCH POP • Lyrics p. 154
"Life in Cyberspace"

DIGITAL SONG   DIGITAL KARAOKE

WRITING BOOSTER p. 151
• Organizing ideas
• Guidance for this writing exercise

ORAL REVIEW

CONTEST Look at the photos for one minute. Then close your books. Who can name all the computer parts and activities in the photos? For example:

There's a printer and . . . OR
He's trying to print photos . . .

PAIR WORK

1 Create a conversation for the man and the woman. They are troubleshooting a problem. Start like this:
Could you take a look at this?

2 Create a conversation for the two men. One is asking for a product recommendation. Start like this:
I'm thinking about getting a new . . .

3 Create a conversation for the two women on the phone. One is asking the other about what she is doing on the computer. Start like this:
Am I interrupting you?

NOW I CAN

☐ Troubleshoot a problem.
☐ Compare product features.
☐ Describe how I use the Internet.
☐ Discuss the impact of the Internet.

PREVIEW

MORAL DILEMMAS
What should they do?

A **GROUP WORK** Have you ever been faced with a moral dilemma similar to the ones in the pictures? Tell your classmates what happened.

B ▶5:18 **PHOTO STORY** Read and listen to a conversation about a moral dilemma.

Matt: I can't believe it! I just picked this up to look at it and the thing broke in two. And with these ridiculous prices, it's going to cost me an arm and a leg.

Noah: Oh, forget it. I'll bet it was already broken.

Matt: You're probably right.

Noah: Just put it back on the shelf. The place is empty. No one saw. Let's just split.

Matt: I couldn't do that.

Noah: Why not? You said it yourself. The prices are ridiculous.

Matt: Well, put yourself in the owner's shoes. Suppose the plate were yours? How would you feel if someone broke it and didn't tell you?

Noah: Well I'm *not* the owner. And, anyway, for him it would be just a drop in the bucket. To *you* it's a lot of money.

Matt: Maybe so. But if I ran out without telling him, I couldn't face myself.

C **FOCUS ON LANGUAGE** Match each idiom from the Photo Story with its meaning.

1 an arm and a leg
2 split
3 put yourself in someone's shoes
4 a drop in the bucket
5 I couldn't face myself.

a a small amount of money
b I would feel bad about it.
c a lot of money
d imagine another person's point of view
e leave

D **THINK AND EXPLAIN** Answer the following questions. Support your answers with quotations from the Photo Story.

1 Does Noah think Matt broke the plate?
2 Why does Noah think it would be easy to leave without saying anything?
3 What does Matt want to do about the plate?

SPEAKING

A **SURVEY** Look at "Moral Dilemmas" and the Photo Story again. Do you agree with the statements below? Circle <u>yes</u> or <u>no</u>, and then give a reason for your answers.

1 Andrew should buy the chocolate with the lower price.	yes / no	
2 Victoria should keep the watch.	yes / no	
3 Amber should tell the waiter there's a mistake.	yes / no	
4 Daniel should send the second jacket back.	yes / no	
5 Matt should tell the store owner what happened.	yes / no	

B **GROUP WORK** Form small groups. Compare your answers and explain your reasons.

GOAL Discuss ethical choices

GRAMMAR *The unreal conditional*

Remember: Conditional sentences express the results of actions or conditions. The real conditional expresses the results of real conditions—conditions that exist.
If I don't use English in class, I won't learn to speak it.

Meaning

Unreal conditional sentences describe the results of unreal conditions—conditions that don't exist.

unreal action or condition	result (if it were true)
If I found a wallet in the street,	I'd try to return it. (unreal: I haven't found one.)

Contraction
would → 'd

Formation

In the *if* clause, use the simple past tense. For the verb <u>be</u>, always use <u>were</u>.
In the result clause, use <u>would</u> + a base form.

unreal action or condition	result (if it were true)
If I had to make a hard decision,	I would try to do the right thing
If she knew how to speak French,	she'd help them.
If you broke something in a store,	would you pay for it?
If you were Matt,	what would you do?
If I were you,	I wouldn't do that.
If you weren't my friend,	I wouldn't tell you what happened.

Be careful!
Don't use <u>would</u> in the *if* clause.
If I knew his name, I would tell you.
NOT If I <s>would know</s> his name . . .

Note: In real and unreal conditional sentences, the clauses can occur in either order. Use a comma if the *if* clause comes first.
If I knew, I would tell you. OR I would tell you if I knew.

GRAMMAR BOOSTER p. 140
Expressing ethics and obligation: expansion
• <u>should</u>, <u>ought to</u>, <u>had better</u>
• <u>have to</u>, <u>must</u>, <u>be supposed to</u>

A **UNDERSTAND THE GRAMMAR** Check the conditional sentences that describe an unreal condition.

☐ 1 If we ate in a restaurant, I would pay the bill.
☐ 2 I'll pay the bill if we eat in a restaurant.
☐ 3 If you get a haircut, you'll look younger.
☐ 4 His wife would worry if he came home really late.
☐ 5 If I were you, I'd tell him the truth.
☐ 6 If I have problem with my office computer, I always ask my co-worker Jim to help.
☐ 7 If they sent me the wrong pants, I would return them.

B **GRAMMAR PRACTICE** Complete each unreal conditional sentence with the correct forms of the verbs.

1 If they .... the wrong price on the coat, ... you .... it without telling
  put .... *buy*
  the clerk?

2 I'm sure you .... something if the restaurant check .... wrong.
  say .... *be*

3 If I .... an expensive piece of jewelry in a public bathroom and .... find the owner,
  find .... *can not*
  I .... it.
  not keep

4 If you .... friends with someone who did something wrong, ... you ....
  be .... *say*
  something to him or her?

5 If you .... two tickets, ... you .... one to a friend?
  have .... *give*

6 What .... if it .... here tomorrow?
  happen .... *snow*

7 They .... to India if they .... the money.
  go .... *have*

8 If you .... two jackets instead of the one you ordered, ... you .... one
  receive .... *send*
  of them back?

9 If they .... here, I .... them what happened.
  be .... *tell*

CONVERSATION MODEL

A ▶5:19 Read and listen to people discussing an ethical choice.

A: Look at this. They didn't charge us for the desserts.

B: Really? I think we'd better tell the waiter.

A: You think so?

B: Absolutely. If we didn't tell him, it would be wrong.

B ▶5:20 **RHYTHM AND INTONATION** Listen again and repeat. Then practice the Conversation Model with a partner.

▶5:21 **Express an ethical obligation**

We'd better tell	
We should tell	the waiter.
We ought to tell	

 PRONUNCIATION *Blending of d + y in would you*

A ▶5:22 Notice how the /d/ and /y/ sounds blend to /dʒ/ in questions with "would you." Read and listen. Then listen again and repeat.

1 What would you do if the waiter didn't charge you for the dessert?

2 What would you do if you found a wallet on the street?

3 Who would you call if you were sick?

4 Where would you go if you wanted a great meal?

B **PAIR WORK** Complete the following questions. Ask a partner the questions, using blending with would you. Then answer your partner's questions.

1 What would you do if .... ?

2 Where would you go if .... ?

3 What would you say if .... ?

NOW YOU CAN Discuss ethical choices

A **CONVERSATION ACTIVATOR** With a partner, change the Conversation Model. Discuss ethical choices, using the situations in the pictures. Then change roles.

A: Look .... They ....
B: .... ? I think .... 'd better ....
A: You think so?
B: Absolutely. If .... , ...

DON'T STOP!
• Say more.

 RECYCLE THIS LANGUAGE.

I couldn't face myself.
Put yourself in [his / her / their] shoes.
If you don't tell the [clerk], [she'll have to pay for it].
If [he didn't charge us], [we would tell him].

▶5:23 **Situations that require an ethical choice**

They didn't charge us for the cake.   They undercharged me.

They gave me too much change.   They gave me more than I ordered.

B **DISCUSSION** Tell your classmates about an ethical choice you had to make in the past.

GOAL Return someone else's property

CONVERSATION MODEL

A ▶5:24 Read and listen to a conversation about returning property.

A: Excuse me. I think you forgot something.

B: I did?

A: Isn't this jacket hers?

B: Oh, you're right. It is. That's nice of you.

A: Don't mention it.

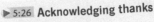
▶5:26 **Acknowledging thanks**
Don't mention it.
My pleasure.
You're welcome.
Not at all.

B ▶5:25 **RHYTHM AND INTONATION** Listen again and repeat. Then practice the Conversation Model with a partner.

GRAMMAR *Possessive pronouns / <u>Whose</u>*

Possessive pronouns can replace nouns and noun phrases. They answer questions with <u>Whose</u> and clarify answers to questions with <u>Which</u>.

A: **Whose** coat is that?   B: It's **mine**. (= It's my coat.)
A: **Which** is <u>her cup</u>?   B: This one is **hers**.

subject pronouns	possessive adjectives	possessive pronouns	
I	my	mine	That's <u>my jacket</u>. / It's **mine**.
you	your	yours	<u>Your dinner</u> was great. / **Yours** was great.
he	his	his	Are these <u>his keys</u>? / Are these **his**?
she	her	hers	She drives <u>her car</u> to work. / She drives **hers** to work.
we	our	ours	These are <u>our shoes</u>. / These are **ours**.
they	their	theirs	They finished <u>their assignment</u>. / They finished **theirs**.

Be careful!
• Don't use a possessive adjective in place of a possessive pronoun.
  Is this **yours**? NOT Is this ~~your~~?
• Don't use a noun after a possessive pronoun.
  These shoes are **mine**. NOT These are ~~mine shoes~~.

GRAMMAR BOOSTER p. 141
• Possessive nouns: review and expansion
• Pronouns: summary

A **GRAMMAR PRACTICE** Replace the noun phrases with possessive pronouns.

1 Those gloves are ~~my gloves~~. *mine*

2 That is ~~her coat~~.

3 The books on that table are ~~Mr. Davison's~~.

4 Their car and ~~our car~~ are parked on the same street.

5 Are those my tickets or ~~her tickets~~?

6 The white house is ~~my mother's house~~.

7 Is this painting ~~your painting~~ or ~~her brother's painting~~?

8 The newspaper under the chair is ~~his daughter's paper~~.

9 Is this DVD ~~your DVD~~ or ~~your friends'~~?

10 Are these ~~your son's shoes~~?

B GRAMMAR PRACTICE Complete the conversations. Circle the correct adjectives and pronouns.

1 A: Whose umbrella is this, (he / his) or (her / hers)?
   B: I'm not sure. Ask them if it's (their / theirs).

2 A: Who is more conservative about clothes? Your parents or your husband's parents?
   B: (He / His), I think. (My / Mine) parents are pretty liberal.

3 A: Is this (ours / our) suitcase?
   B: No, I already got (our / ours) suitcase, so this one can't be (our / ours).

4 A: I found this necklace near Carrie's desk. Is it (her / hers)?
   B: No, it's (my / mine) necklace. I'm so happy someone found it!

5 A: Is that (their / theirs) car?
   B: No, (their / theirs) is the black one over there.

6 A: Where should we meet? At (your / yours) house or (my / mine)?
   B: Neither. Let's meet at (my / mine) office.

C ▶ 5:27 **LISTEN TO ACTIVATE GRAMMAR** Listen to the conversations and complete each statement with a possessive pronoun.

1 The bag is ....

2 The phone is .... , but the keys belong to Brad's wife. They're ....

3 The coat isn't ....

4 The concert tickets aren't ....

NOW YOU CAN **Return someone else's property**

A CONVERSATION ACTIVATOR With a partner, change the Conversation Model to role-play returning the items in the pictures. Then change roles.

   A: Excuse me. I think you forgot something.
   B: I did?
   A: .... yours?
   B: Oh, you're right. .... That's nice of you.
   A: ....

B GROUP WORK First, collect personal items from your classmates. Then role-play returning someone else's property. Walk around the room to find the owners. Use possessive pronouns.

C EXTENSION Place all your classmates' personal items on a table. Ask about each item. Identify the owner, using possessive pronouns.

   " Whose phone is this? "

   " It's his. "

BEFORE YOU LISTEN

EXPLORE YOUR IDEAS Which actions would be OK, and which wouldn't be OK for the following people: you? your parents? your grandparents? your own teenaged child?

> " It wouldn't be OK if my grandmother pierced her nose. Face piercing is for young people. She's too old. "

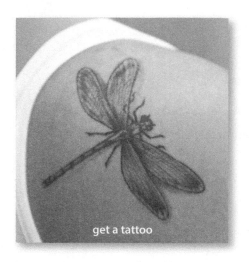

get a tattoo

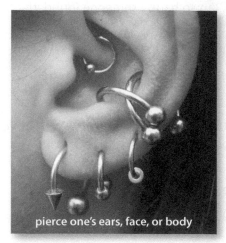

pierce one's ears, face, or body

dye one's hair a wild color

LISTENING COMPREHENSION

A ▶5:28 **LISTEN FOR MAIN IDEAS** Listen to each conversation. Then circle the correct word or phrase to complete each statement.

1 a Beth thinks it's (OK / not OK) to wear an earring to the office.

 b Beth (convinces / doesn't convince) Luke.

2 a Celia's husband thinks it's (OK / wrong) for a woman to have a tattoo.

 b Celia's husband thinks it's (OK / wrong) for a man to have a tattoo.

3 a The first man is (happy / not happy) that his daughter is going to law school.

 b He wants his daughter to (stay home / work).

4 a Kate's dad is (worried / not worried) about what people think of Kate.

 b Kate is (worried / not worried) about what people think of her.

B **UNDERSTAND VOCABULARY FROM CONTEXT** Read the following quotations from the conversations. Then choose the meaning of each underlined word or phrase. Listen again if necessary.

1 "But lots of people are <u>old-fashioned</u>, and they don't think men should wear earrings."

 a preferring the way things were in the past
 b preferring the way things are now

2 "What a <u>double standard</u>!"

 a having the same rules for everyone
 b having different rules for different people

3 "That's a little <u>sexist</u>, if you ask me!"

 a not treating men and women in the same way
 b treating men and women in the same way

4 "But <u>modesty</u> is very important for girls."

 a wearing clothes that cover one's body
 b wearing clothes that show one's body

C **APPLY NEW VOCABULARY** Write an example for each word or phrase from your own experience. Compare examples with a partner.

> ❝ I think an example of old-fashioned is not letting teenagers go out on dates. ❞

old-fashioned	
a double standard	
sexist	
modesty	

D **PAIR WORK** Discuss the picture. Use the following words and phrases in your discussion: <u>old-fashioned</u>, <u>sexist</u>, <u>double standard</u>, <u>modesty</u>.

> ❝ He's measuring the woman's swimsuit. If she were a man, he wouldn't measure it. That's a double standard. ❞

Man measuring the length of a woman's swimsuit (U.S., 1920s)

NOW YOU CAN Express personal values

A **IDEA FRAMING** Complete the Values Self-Test. Then compare answers with a partner. Do you have the same values?

Values Self-Test

Check the boxes that best describe your values. Include a specific example.

1. ❏ I'm modern in my attitudes about modesty.
   ❏ I'm old-fashioned in my attitudes about modesty.
   Explain. _____
   _____
   _____

2. ❏ I think tattoos and body piercing are OK for men.
   ❏ I think tattoos and body piercing are OK for women.
   Explain. _____
   _____
   _____

3. ❏ I think it's OK to have a double standard for different people.
   ❏ I think the rules should be the same for everyone.
   Explain. _____
   _____
   _____

4. ❏ Some people might say I'm sexist.
   ❏ Nobody would say I'm sexist.
   Explain. _____
   _____
   _____

B **NOTEPADDING** Answer each question and explain your opinion, using examples.

Is it sometimes OK to have a double standard for men and women?
Can people be sexist when they talk about men, or only about women?
Are old-fashioned ideas usually better or worse than modern ideas?

C **GROUP WORK** Now discuss each question, expressing your personal values. Expect people to disagree with you!

🔁 **RECYCLE THIS LANGUAGE.**

Agreement and disagreement	Likes and dislikes	Adjectives
I agree.	I like __.	liberal
I disagree.	I dislike __.	conservative
It depends.	I hate __.	strict
	I can't stand __.	modest
	I don't mind __.	
	__ drives me crazy!	

BEFORE YOU READ

PREDICT Look at the headlines of the three news stories. In what way do you think the stories will be similar?

READING ▶ 5:29

Homeless Man Returns Wallet with $900
Posted on: Monday, 17 April

SANTA ANA, Calif. - A homeless man searching through trash bins for recyclable cans found a missing wallet and returned it to its owner. Kim Bogue, who works in the city, realized that her wallet was missing last week and doubted she'd ever get back the $900 and credit cards inside. "I prayed that night and asked God to help me," said Bogue, who was saving the money for a trip to her native Thailand.

Days later, a homeless man found the wallet wrapped in a plastic bag in the trash, where Bogue had accidentally thrown it away with her lunch. He gave it to Sherry Wesley, who works in a nearby building. "He came to me with the wad of money and said, 'This probably belongs to someone that you work with. Can you return it?'" Wesley said.

"He has a very good heart," said Bogue, who gave the man a $100 reward. "If someone else had found it, the money would have been gone."

Man Risks Life to Save Another

Many people who ride a busy urban subway wonder, "What would happen if I fell off the platform and onto the tracks? What would I do?" Others wonder, "What would I do if someone else fell?"

That question was answered in a split-second decision made by "subway hero" Wesley Autrey, a fifty-year-old New York City construction worker on his way to work. Autrey jumped onto the tracks to save a fellow passenger from an oncoming New York City subway train.

The passenger, Cameron Hollopeter, 20, a film student at the New York Film Academy, had fallen between the tracks after suffering a seizure. Autrey rolled Hollopeter into a gap between the rails and covered him with his own body just as the train entered the station. Both men survived.

"I don't feel like I did something spectacular; I just saw someone who needed help," Mr. Autrey said. "I did what I felt was right."

An act of honesty by airport screener

NEW DELHI: In a display of honesty, a security agent at the Indira Gandhi International Airport handed over a small plastic bag with US $3,000 in cash to a passenger who had completely forgotten the bag after it passed through the airport screening machine.

Noticing that the bag had been left behind, Dalbir Singh made an announcement asking passengers to come forward to claim it. However, when no one claimed it, Singh inspected the baggage tag and guessed it probably belonged to a passenger en route to Mumbai. An announcement was made on the next flight to Mumbai, and the owner of the bag came forward to collect it.

Singh was given a cash reward for his honesty.

A **SUMMARIZE** Summarize one of the articles. Close your book and tell the story in your own words.

B **INTERPRET INFORMATION** Discuss each person's motives for his or her actions.

  1 Why did Kim Bogue give the homeless man a reward?

  2 Why did Wesley Autrey risk his life to save a stranger?

  3 Why do you think Dalbir Singh returned the money to the passenger?

C **RELATE TO PERSONAL EXPERIENCE** Think of a story you have heard about someone who helped a stranger in need. Tell it to the class.

A **NOTEPADDING** Answer the questions about each situation.

Situation: Someone ahead of you at a coffee bar has paid for your coffee.

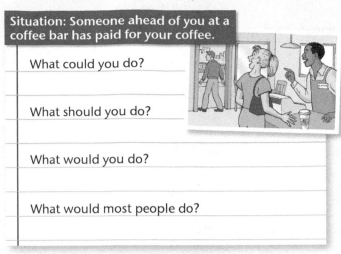

What could you do?

What should you do?

What would you do?

What would most people do?

Situation: A blind man is crossing a street in front of you and a car is coming.

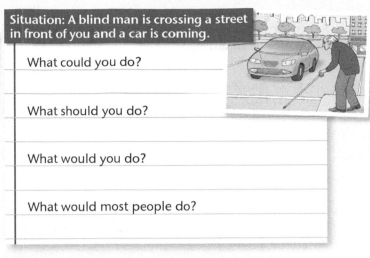

What could you do?

What should you do?

What would you do?

What would most people do?

Situation: You find a wallet full of cash in a restaurant.

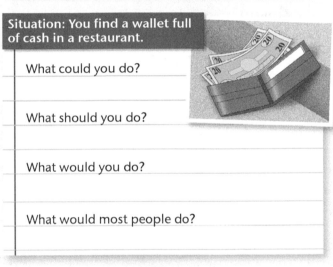

What could you do?

What should you do?

What would you do?

What would most people do?

Situation: You find cash at an ATM.

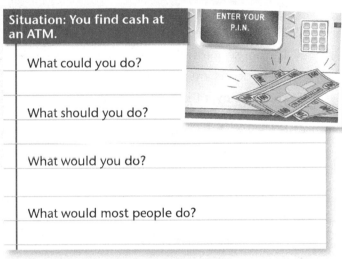

What could you do?

What should you do?

What would you do?

What would most people do?

Situation: The cashier undercharges you.

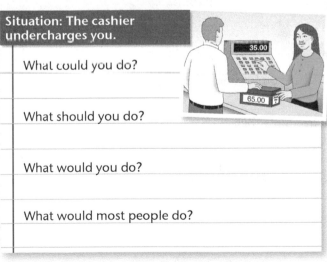

What could you do?

What should you do?

What would you do?

What would most people do?

Situation: You find a gold watch in a department store dressing room.

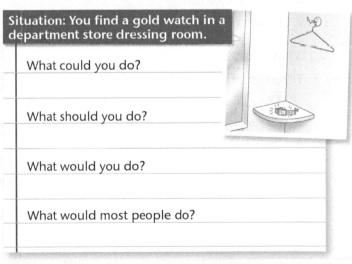

What could you do?

What should you do?

What would you do?

What would most people do?

B **GROUP WORK** Compare your notes. Would you all do the same things in these situations? Use the unreal conditional and expressions from the Photo Story on page 111.

> If I found cash near an ATM, I would keep it. There would be no way to find the owner.

Text-mining (optional)
Find and underline three words or phrases in the Reading that were new to you. Use them in your Group Work
    For example: "a split-second decision."

REVIEW

A ▶5:30 Listen to the conversations. Check <u>Yes</u> or <u>No</u> to answer each question and explain your answers.

	Yes	No
1 Do you think John has a double standard?	☐	☐
Explain your answer: ....
2 Do you think Jessica's mom is sexist?	☐	☐
Explain your answer: ....
3 Do you think Alex's dad is old-fashioned?	☐	☐
Explain your answer: ....

B Complete the questions with <u>Whose</u>. Then answer each question, using possessive pronouns. Follow the example.

1 Those shoes belong to my daughter. ....*Whose are*.... they? ....*They're hers.*....

2 That sweater belongs to my son. .... it? ....

3 The house across the street is my parents' house. .... it? ....

4 These tickets are my husband's and mine. .... they? ....

5 The table over there is your table. .... it? ....

C Complete each conditional sentence in your own words.

1 If the weather were good, ...

2 If .... , I'd go out to eat tonight.

3 If I found your wallet, ...

4 If .... , I'd call home.

5 I'd be angry with my children if ....

6 If I had a new car, ...

7 I would choose a new career if ....

For additional language practice . . .

♫ TOP NOTCH POP • Lyrics p. 154
"What Would You Do?"

DIGITAL SONG   DIGITAL KARAOKE

D What would you do? Complete each unreal conditional sentence.

1 You order two sandwiches for lunch, but they only charge you for one.

YOU ⟩ "If the restaurant undercharged me, I ...."

2 You pay for a newspaper that costs one dollar with a five-dollar bill. The merchant gives you nine dollars change.

YOU ⟩ "If the merchant gave me too much change, I ...."

3 You buy a smart phone from a website. When the package arrives, you see that the company has sent you two MP3 players and the smart phone.

YOU ⟩ "If the company sent me more items than I paid for, I ...."

WRITING

Write three paragraphs about Matt's dilemma in the Photo Story on page 111. In the first paragraph, summarize the situation. In the second paragraph, write about what Matt could or should do. In the third paragraph, write what you would do if you were Matt. Explain your reasons, using the unreal conditional.

WRITING BOOSTER p. 152
• Introducing conflicting ideas
• Guidance for this writing exercise

ORAL REVIEW

CONTEST Form teams. With your team, look at the two pictures for one minute. Then close your books and tell the story you saw in the pictures. The team that remembers more details wins.

PAIR WORK

1 Tell your partner what you would do if you were the woman who found the lost object. Use the unreal conditional. Start like this:

If I found . . . , I would . . .

2 Create a conversation for the people in the second picture. Use possessive pronouns. Start like this:

Excuse me. Is this your . . .

A few minutes later

GATE 22 B

departures

NOW I CAN

☐ Discuss ethical choices.
☐ Return someone else's property.
☐ Express personal values.
☐ Discuss acts of kindness and honesty.

Reference Charts

PRONUNCIATION TABLE

Vowels

Symbol	Key Words
i	beat, feed
ɪ	bit, did
eɪ	date, paid
ɛ	bet, bed
æ	bat, bad
ɑ	box, odd, father
ɔ	bought, dog
oʊ	boat, road
ʊ	book, good
u	boot, food, flu
ʌ	but, mud, mother
ə	banana, among
ɚ	shirt, murder
aɪ	bite, cry, buy, eye
aʊ	about, how
ɔɪ	voice, boy
ɪr	deer
ɛr	bare
ɑr	bar
ɔr	door
ʊr	tour

Consonants

Symbol	Key Words	Symbol	Key Words
p	pack, happy	z	zip, please, goes
b	back, rubber	ʃ	ship, machine, station, special, discussion
t	tie		
d	die	ʒ	measure, vision
k	came, key, quick	h	hot, who
g	game, guest	m	men
tʃ	church, nature, watch	n	sun, know, pneumonia
dʒ	judge, general, major	ŋ	sung, ringing
f	fan, photograph	w	wet, white
v	van	l	light, long
θ	thing, breath	r	right, wrong
ð	then, breathe	y	yes
s	sip, city, psychology		
ţ	butter, bottle		
t˺	button		

IRREGULAR VERBS

base form	simple past	past participle	base form	simple past	past participle
be	was / were	been	leave	left	left
become	became	become	let	let	let
begin	began	begun	lose	lost	lost
break	broke	broken	make	made	made
bring	brought	brought	mean	meant	meant
build	built	built	meet	met	met
buy	bought	bought	pay	paid	paid
catch	caught	caught	put	put	put
choose	chose	chosen	quit	quit	quit
come	came	come	read /rid/	read /rɛd/	read /rɛd/
cost	cost	cost	ride	rode	ridden
cut	cut	cut	ring	rang	rung
do	did	done	rise	rose	risen
draw	drew	drawn	run	ran	run
dream	dreamed / dreamt	dreamed / dreamt	say	said	said
drink	drank	drunk	see	saw	seen
drive	drove	driven	sell	sold	sold
eat	ate	eaten	send	sent	sent
fall	fell	fallen	shake	shook	shaken
feed	fed	fed	sing	sang	sung
feel	felt	felt	sit	sat	sat
fight	fought	fought	sleep	slept	slept
find	found	found	speak	spoke	spoken
fit	fit	fit	spend	spent	spent
fly	flew	flown	stand	stood	stood
forget	forgot	forgotten	steal	stole	stolen
get	got	gotten	swim	swam	swum
give	gave	given	take	took	taken
go	went	gone	teach	taught	taught
grow	grew	grown	tell	told	told
have	had	had	think	thought	thought
hear	heard	heard	throw	threw	thrown
hit	hit	hit	understand	understood	understood
hold	held	held	wake up	woke up	woken up
hurt	hurt	hurt	wear	wore	worn
keep	kept	kept	win	won	won
know	knew	known	write	wrote	written

1 THE PRESENT OF BE

Statements

I	am	
You We They	are	late.
He She It	is	

2 THE SIMPLE PRESENT TENSE

Statements

I You We They	speak English.
He She	speaks English.

Yes / no questions

Do	I you we they	know them?
Does	he she it	eat meat?

Short answers

Yes,	I you we they	do.		No,	I you we they	don't.
	he she it	does.			he she it	doesn't.

Information questions

What do	you we they	need?
When does	he she it	start?
Who	wants needs likes	this book?

3 THE PRESENT CONTINUOUS

Statements

I	am	watching TV.
You We They	are	studying English.
He She It	is	arriving now.

Yes / no questions

Am	I	
Are	you we they	going too fast?
Is	he she it	

Short answers

Yes,	I	am.		No,	I'm not.
	you	are.			you aren't / you're not.
	he she it	is.			he isn't / he's not. she isn't / she's not. it isn't / it's not.
	we they	are.			we aren't / we're not. they aren't / they're not.

Information questions

What	are	you we they	doing?
When	is	he she it	leaving?
Where	am	I	staying tonight?
Who	is		driving?

4 THE PAST OF BE

Statements

I He She It	was late.
We You They	were early.

(The past of be–continued)

Yes / no questions

Was	I he she it	on time?
Were	we you they	in the same class?

Short answers

Yes,	I he she it	was.
	we you they	were.

No,	I he she it	wasn't.
	we you they	weren't.

Information questions

Where	were	we? you? they?
When	was	he she it	here?
Who	were	they?
Who	was	he? she? it?

5 THE SIMPLE PAST TENSE

Many verbs are irregular in the simple past tense.
See the list of irregular verbs on page 123.

Statements

I You He She It We They	stopped working.

I You He She It We They	didn't start again.

Yes / no questions

Did	I you he she it we they	make a good dinner?

Short answers

Yes,	I you he she it we they	did.

No,	I you he she it we they	didn't.

Information questions

When did	I you he she it we they	read that?
Who		called?

6 THE FUTURE WITH BE GOING TO

Statements

I'm You're He's She's It's We're They're	going to	be here soon.

I'm You're He's She's It's We're They're	not going to	be here soon.

Yes / no questions

Are	you we they	going to want coffee?
Am	I	going to be late?
Is	he she it	going to arrive on time?

Short answers

Yes,	I	am.
	you	are.
	he she it	is.
	we they	are.

No,	I'm not. you aren't / you're not. he isn't / he's not. she isn't / she's not. it isn't / it's not. we aren't / we're not. they aren't / they're not.

Information questions

What	are	you we they	going to see?
When	is	he she it	going to shop?
Where	am	I	going to stay tomorrow?
Who	is		going to call?

TOP NOTCH 2B

Grammar Booster

Use to / used to: use and form

Use to and **used to** express a past habitual action, but one that is no longer true today.
> When I was a kid, I **didn't use to eat** vegetables. But now I do.

Remember: In **yes** / **no** questions and negative statements, use **use to** NOT **used to**.
> I **used to** stay up late. Now I don't.
> I **didn't use to** (NOT ~~used to~~) get up early. Now I do.
> **Did** you **use to** (NOT ~~used to~~) go dancing more often?

> **Note:** The simple past tense can express a past habitual action if there is a reference to a period of time in the past.
> When I was a kid, I **didn't eat** peppers. I still don't today.

A On a separate sheet of paper, change each statement into a **yes** / **no** question.

> I used to go running every day. *Did you use to go running every day?*

1 There used to be a large tree in front of your house.
2 Mr. and Mrs. Palmer used to go dancing every weekend.
3 Their grandmother used to put sugar in their orange juice.
4 Luke used to be very overweight.

B On a separate sheet of paper, use the prompts to write logical sentences with negative or affirmative forms of **use to** / **used to**.

1 Jason and Trish / get lots of exercise, but now they go swimming every day.
2 There / be a movie theater on Smith Street, but now there isn't.
3 No one / worry about fatty foods, but now most people do.
4 English / be an international language, but now everyone uses English to communicate around the world.
5 Women in North America / wear pants, but now it's very common for them to wear them.

Be used to / get used to

Be used to + a noun phrase means to be accustomed to something. Compare **use to** / **used to** with **be used to**.
> I **didn't use to like** spicy food. But now I do. (**used to** + base form)
> I'm **used to the noise** now. But at first, it really bothered me. (**be used to** + a noun phrase)

Get used to + a noun phrase means to become accustomed to something.
> You'll **get used to the new menu** after a few days.

Be careful! With **be used to**, don't change **used** in negative statements or questions.
> He **wasn't used to** the weather there. NOT He wasn't ~~use to~~ . . .
> **Are** you **used to** life here? NOT Are you ~~use to~~ . . .

C Check the sentences in which **used to** means "accustomed to something."

☐ 1 When the school term ended, I was finally used to the new teacher.
☐ 2 In our other class, the teacher used to be very strict.
☐ 3 They used to like red meat, but now they don't.
☐ 4 Because we lived in the mountains, we weren't used to fresh seafood.
☐ 5 I'm sure she'll get used to her new apartment soon.
☐ 6 These shoes used to be comfortable, but now they're too loose.
☐ 7 I'm sure she'll get used to wearing high-heeled shoes.

D Write ✓ if the sentence is correct. Write ✗ if it is incorrect and make corrections.

☐ 1 I'll never get use to the traffic here.
☐ 2 We didn't use to take vacations very often.
☐ 3 Is he use to his new roommate yet?
☐ 4 Will she ever get use to life in the city?
☐ 5 What did you used to do on weekdays when you weren't working?

E On a separate sheet of paper, write two sentences about something you're used to and two sentences about something you're not used to.

Repeated actions in the past: *would* + *base form*

You can also use <u>would</u> + the base form of a verb to describe repeated past actions. In this use, <u>would</u> has the same meaning as <u>used to</u>.

When we were young, our parents would go camping with us. (= used to go camping with us.)

Be careful! With non-action verbs that don't describe repeated actions, use <u>used to</u>, not <u>would</u>.

I used to have a lot of clothes. NOT I ~~would have~~ a lot of clothes.
My hometown used to be Dakar. NOT My hometown ~~would be~~ Dakar.
I used to be a terrible English student. NOT I ~~would be~~ a terrible English student.
My friends and I used to hate baseball. NOT My friends and I ~~would hate~~ baseball.

F If it is possible, complete the sentence with <u>would</u>. If not, use a form of <u>used to</u>.

1 They .... go to the beach every Saturday in the summer.

2 I .... have a really large kitchen in my old house.

3 My husband never .... like coffee, but now he can't get enough of it.

4 Almost every evening of our vacation we .... eat at a terrific outdoor restaurant.

5 Before the microwave, people .... heat up soup on the top of the stove.

6 Sigrid .... be a tour guide, but now she's a professional chef.

7 There .... be three or four Italian restaurants in town, but now there aren't any.

UNIT 6 *Lesson 2*

Negative *yes* / *no* questions: short answers

Answer negative <u>yes</u> / <u>no</u> questions the same way as you would answer affirmative <u>yes</u> / <u>no</u> questions.

Is Jane a vegetarian?
Isn't Jane a vegetarian? | Yes, she is. / No, she isn't.

Do they have two sons?
Don't they have two sons? | Yes, they do. / No, they don't.

Answer each negative question with a short answer. (Use the information for your answer.)

1 A: Isn't Jeremy a lawyer?
   B: .... He's not a lawyer.

2 A: Doesn't Bob have two brothers?
   B: .... He has two younger brothers.

3 A: Haven't you been to Siberia before?
   B: .... I've never been here before.

4 A: Aren't you learning English right now?
   B: .... I'm studying English at the institute.

5 A: Wasn't Nancy at the movies last night?
   B: .... She didn't go to the movies.

6 A: Don't Sachiko and Tomofumi have a car?
   B: .... They own a minivan.

Gerunds and infinitives: usage within sentences

Gerunds (-ing form of a verb) and infinitives (to + base form) function as nouns within sentences.

Gerunds
Like nouns, gerunds can be subjects, subject complements, direct objects, and objects of prepositions.
Painting is my favorite leisure-time activity. (subject)
My favorite activity is painting. (subject complement; usually follows <u>be</u>)
I enjoy painting. (direct object)
I read a book about the history of painting. (object of the preposition <u>of</u>)

Infinitives
Infinitives can be subjects, subject complements, and direct objects.
To paint well is a talent. (subject)
The only thing he needs is to paint. (subject complement; usually follows <u>be</u>)
I want to paint. (direct object)

Underline the gerunds and circle the infinitives in these sentences. How is each used in the sentence? On the line next to each sentence, write *S* for subject, *C* for subject complement, *DO* for direct object, or *OP* for object of a preposition.

.... **1** I enjoy watching old movies every night on TV.

.... **2** Her greatest dream was to see all of her children attend college.

.... **3** What's the point of creating a nice environment at home if genetics is the only thing that counts?

.... **4** Avoiding too much pressure helps children become less critical.

.... **5** My niece plans to study personality development next semester.

Negative gerunds

A gerund can be made negative by using a negative word before it.
I like not going to bed too late.
They complained about never having enough time.

Complete the paragraph with affirmative and negative gerunds.

I really want to do something to improve my appearance and lose weight. I'm sick of .... able to fit into my
                                                                                              1 be
clothes. I know it's not enough to complain about .... weight—I need to do something about it! I plan to spend
                                                                    2 gain
every afternoon .... my bike. Also, I want to go on a diet, but I'm afraid of .... hungry all the time.
                      3 ride   4 feel
I worry about .... enough energy to exercise if I'm .... enough to eat.
                    5 have   6 get

The passive voice: transitive verbs and intransitive verbs

A transitive verb can have a direct object. Transitive verbs can be used in the active voice or passive voice.

active voice	passive voice
Picasso painted *Guernica* in 1937. →	*Guernica* was painted in 1937.

An intransitive verb cannot have a direct object. With an intransitive verb, there is no "receiver" of an action.

The painting arrives tomorrow.
The *Mona Lisa* will stay at the Louvre.
That new sculpture looks like a Botero.

Remember: The subject of a sentence performs the action of the verb. A direct object receives the action of the verb.

Common intransitive verbs

arrive	happen	sit
come	laugh	sleep
die	live	stand
fall	rain	stay
go	seem	walk

A Check each sentence that has an intransitive verb.

☐ 1 Pedro Almodóvar's new film arrives in theaters this fall.

☐ 2 A Canadian art collector has bought two of Michelangelo's drawings.

☐ 3 Someone stole Edvard Munch's painting *The Scream* in 2004.

☐ 4 The painter Georgia O'Keeffe lived in the southwestern part of the United States.

☐ 5 The Van Gogh Museum in Amsterdam sent *Sunflowers* on a world tour.

☐ 6 The traveling collection of ancient Roman sculpture is coming to San Diego this week.

☐ 7 The Metropolitan Museum of Art opened a new gallery last year.

The passive voice: form

Form the passive voice with a form of <u>be</u> and the past participle of a verb.

	Active voice	Passive voice
Simple present tense	Art collectors buy famous paintings all over the world.	Famous paintings are bought by art collectors all over the world.
Present continuous	The Film Center is showing Kurosawa's films.	Kurosawa's films are being shown at the Film Center.
Present perfect	Some world leaders have bought Yu Hung's paintings.	Yu Hung's paintings have been bought by some world leaders.
Simple past tense	I. M. Pei designed the Grand Pyramid at the Louvre.	The Grand Pyramid at the Louvre was designed by I. M. Pei.
Past continuous	In 2010, the museum was selling copies of Monet's paintings.	In 2010, copies of Monet's paintings were being sold by the museum.
Future with <u>will</u>	Ang Lee will direct a new film next year.	A new film will be directed by Ang Lee next year.
Future with <u>be going to</u>	The Tate Modern is going to show Van Gogh's drawings next month.	Van Gogh's drawings are going to be shown at the Tate Modern next month.

B On a separate sheet of paper, rewrite each sentence in the passive voice. Use a <u>by</u> phrase only if it is important to know who is performing the action.

1 Someone actually stole the *Mona Lisa* in 1911.

2 Paloma Picasso designed these pieces of silver jewelry.

3 Someone will repair the sculpture when it gets old.

4 People have paid millions of U.S. dollars for some of Van Gogh's paintings.

5 They are showing some new paintings at the Smith Gallery this week.

6 The Malcolm Museum is going to exhibit ten sculptures by Asian artists.

7 Frida Kahlo was painting these pieces while she was sick in bed.

8 People built great pyramids throughout Central America during the height of the Mayan civilization.

C On a separate sheet of paper, rewrite the sentences in Exercise A that have a transitive verb, changing the active voice to the passive voice.

The passive voice: _yes_ / _no_ questions

To form _yes_ / _no_ questions in the passive voice, move the first auxiliary verb before the subject.

Simple present tense	Are famous paintings ~~are~~ bought by art collectors?
Present continuous	Are Kurosawa's films ~~are~~ being shown at the Film Center?
Present perfect	Have Yu Hung's paintings ~~have~~ been bought by some world leaders?
Simple past tense	Was the Grand Pyramid at the Louvre ~~was~~ designed by I. M. Pei?
Past continuous	Were copies of Monet's paintings ~~were~~ being sold by the museum?
Future with <u>will</u>	Will a new film ~~will~~ be directed by Ang Lee next year?
Future with <u>be going to</u>	Is a collection of Van Gogh's drawings ~~is~~ going to be shown next month?

On a separate sheet of paper, rewrite the sentences as _yes_ / _no_ questions in the passive voice.

1 That new film about families is being directed by Gillian Armstrong.

2 One of da Vinci's most famous drawings has been sold by a German art collector.

3 A rare ceramic figure from the National Palace Museum in Taipei will be sent to the Metropolitan Museum of Art in New York.

4 A new exhibit is going to be opened at the Photography Gallery this week.

5 Some new paintings have been bought by the Prado Museum for their permanent collection.

6 _Las Meninas_ can be seen at the Prado Museum in Madrid.

7 The _Jupiter_ Symphony was written by Mozart.

8 Some of Michelangelo's work was being shown around the world in the 1960s.

UNIT **9** *Lesson 1*

Other ways to express a purpose

<u>In order to</u>

You can use <u>in order to</u> with a base form of a verb to express a purpose. The following three sentences have the same meaning.

I scrolled down in order to read the text.

I scrolled down because I wanted to read the text.

I scrolled down to read the text.

<u>For</u>

You can use <u>for</u> to express a purpose before a noun phrase or gerund phrase.

She e-mailed me for some advice.

They shop online for electronic products.

I use my smart phone for e-mailing clients.

Be careful! Don't use <u>for</u> before an infinitive of purpose.

DON'T SAY She e-mailed me ~~for~~ to ask a question.

A On a separate sheet of paper, rewrite the sentences with <u>in order to</u>.

1 She joined Facebook to meet new people.
2 Jason surfs the Internet to see what's new.
3 Alison uses online banking to pay all her bills.
4 They always print their documents first to read them carefully.
5 I never use the pull-down menu to open files.
6 He used an online telephone service to call his family.

B Complete each sentence with <u>for</u> or <u>to</u>.

1 My friend e-mailed me .... say he's getting married.
2 Jane shops online .... clothing.
3 I went online .... find a new keyboard.
4 Matt created a web page .... keeping in touch with his family and friends.
5 Sometimes I use my computer .... download movies.
6 We both log on to the Internet .... information.
7 Just click the icon .... open the file.
8 When Gina's computer crashed, her brother came over .... help her.

UNIT 9 *Lesson 2*

Comparison with adjectives: review

<u>As . . . as</u>
Use <u>as</u> . . . <u>as</u> to indicate how two things are equal or the same. Use <u>not as</u> . . . <u>as</u> to indicate how two things are different.
The new Jax 10 monitor is just as good as the Jax 20.
The Jax 10 monitor is not as big as the Jax 20.

Comparatives
Use comparatives to show how two things are not equal. Use <u>than</u> if the second item is mentioned.
My laptop is heavier than John's (is).   OR My laptop is heavier.
Regular mail is less convenient than e-mail. OR Regular mail is less convenient.

Superlatives
Use superlatives to show how one thing is different from two or more other things. Remember to use <u>the</u> with the superlative.
The M2, LX, and Bell printers are all good. But the Bell is the best.
The Gatt 40 monitor is the least expensive one you can buy.

A Correct the error in each sentence.

1 The Orca speakers aren't as heavier as the Yaltas.
2 My old laptop didn't have as many problems than my new laptop.
3 I checked out the three top brands, and the Piston was definitely the better.
4 Maxwell's web camera is much more expensive as their digital camera.
5 Of all the monitors I looked at, the X60 is definitely larger.
6 The Jaguar is most powerful computer in the world.

Comparison with adverbs

Comparatives
My new computer runs faster than my old one.
The X20 operates more quietly than the X30.

<u>As . . . as</u>
My new phone works as well as my old one.
The Macro laptop doesn't run as slowly as the Pell does.

Superlatives
Of these three laptops, the MPro starts up the most slowly.

Remember: Adverbs often give information about verbs.
My phone works **well**.   My printer prints **fast**.
Many adjectives can be changed to adverbs by adding -<u>ly</u>.

| loud | ➔ | **loudly** | quick | ➔ | **quickly** | quiet | ➔ | **quietly** |
| poor | ➔ | **poorly** | bad | ➔ | **badly** | slow | ➔ | **slowly** |

B   On a separate sheet of paper, rewrite each pair of sentences into a single sentence using comparatives. Then write single sentences using as . . . as.

1   My brother's smart phone downloads music quickly. My MP3 player doesn't download quickly.
2   My new computer doesn't log on slowly. My old computer logs on slowly.
3   Your old monitor works well. My new monitor doesn't work well.
4   The Rico printer prints quickly. The Grant printer doesn't print quickly.
5   The Pace scanner doesn't run quietly. The Rico scanner runs quietly.

UNIT 10 Lesson 1

Should and ought to; had better

Use should or ought to + a base form to state an opinion or give advice, especially about an ethical choice. Ought to has the same meaning as should, but should is slightly less formal.
    You should (or ought to) return the wallet. You shouldn't keep it.

Use had better + a base form to state an opinion or give stronger advice. The meaning is similar to should and ought to, but had better expresses the idea that there is a consequence for not doing something.
    You'd better tell the waiter that the check is wrong. If you don't, he will have to pay.
    You'd better not eat at the Fairway Café. I got sick there the last time I did.

Remember: Should, ought to, and had better precede other verbs and give them a special meaning. They never change form.

> **Note:** In American English it's very uncommon to use ought to in negative statements or questions. Use should or shouldn't instead.

A   On a separate sheet of paper, complete the statements about an ethical choice, expressing your own ideas.

1   Colleagues in an office should always ....
2   Parents of young children should not ....
3   We ought to tell the store owner when ....
4   You forgot to pay your check? You had better ....
5   We had better not .... It's too expensive.

B   On a separate sheet of paper, write five suggestions to a visitor to your country, using had better or had better not.

> 66 You'd better not take the local train to Bradbury. It's too slow. 99

Have to, must, and be supposed to

Have to and must
Use have to or the modal must + a base form to express obligation when there is no other choice of action available.
    Students must take this exam.
    You have to take the 6:00 train if you want to arrive on time.

Use don't have to (NOT must) to express a lack of obligation.
    You don't have to pay for the shoes if you don't like them. You can return them.

Use must not (NOT don't have to) for a strong or legal prohibition.
    Passengers must not leave their baggage unattended in the waiting area.

Be supposed to
Use be supposed to (or not be supposed to) + a base form to express an expected, but not a required, action. The degree of obligation is weaker than with have to or must.
    We're supposed to pay our check at the front of the coffee shop, not at the table. (The restaurant expects diners to pay at the front.)
    Hotel guests are not supposed to use the towels from their rooms at the pool.

> **Note:** Must is very formal and not very common in speaking. It is generally used by a person in authority (e.g., a teacher or boss) to state policy or law. Have to is much more common in both speaking and writing. The more informal have got to is also common in spoken English.
>   Sorry. I've got to hurry. I'm going to be late.
>
> Don't use must not for a lack of obligation. Use don't have to or doesn't have to.

C On a separate sheet of paper, write each sentence two ways: with <u>must</u> and with <u>have to</u>.

1 Drivers / obey the speed limit.
2 Students / arrive on time for class.
3 In this beach restaurant / diners / wear shoes. If you are barefoot, don't come in.
4 You / have a reservation to eat at the Palace Restaurant.

D On a separate sheet of paper, write five sentences that describe actions your school expects from its students. Use <u>be supposed to</u>.

> Students are supposed to come on time to class. They're not supposed to be late.

E Choose the sentence closer in meaning to each numbered statement or question.

1 Do you think the Milton Restaurant is a good place to eat?
   a Do you think I should eat at the Milton Restaurant?
   b Do you think I have to eat at the Milton Restaurant?

2 If you don't have a reservation, the restaurant won't give you a table.
   a The restaurant is supposed to give you a table.
   b You had better have a reservation.

3 They don't accept credit cards in this store. They only accept cash.
   a You have to pay with cash.
   b You ought to pay with cash.

4 Don't wear shorts in the restaurant.
   a You must not wear shorts in the restaurant.
   b You don't have to wear shorts in the restaurant.

UNIT 10 Lesson 2

Possessive nouns: review and expansion

Add 's (an apostrophe + s) to a name or a singular noun.
Where is Glenn's car?   What's your daughter's married name?
This is Ms. Baker's class.   I love Dickens's novels.

Add an apostrophe to plural nouns that end in s. For irregular plurals, such as <u>women</u> or <u>children</u>, add 's.
the women's room   the boys' clothes   the Jacksons' car

Add 's to the name or noun that comes last in a list of two or more.
Jean and Ralph's house

A Correct the following sentences, adding an apostrophe or an apostrophe + <u>s</u> to the possessive nouns.

Carmen's jacket is under the table.

1 The two girls keys are lost.
2 Mr. Stiller English is really fluent.
3 The doctor office is downstairs.
4 Sarah and Tom children are at the Taylor School.
5 That man car is parked in a no-parking zone.
6 Julia friend brother is going to get married tonight.
7 The Smiths garden is beautiful.

Pronouns: summary

Subject pronouns

Subject pronouns represent subject nouns and noun phrases. The subject pronouns are I, you, he, she, it, we, and they.

> Matt didn't break the plate = He didn't break the plate.

Object pronouns

Object pronouns represent nouns (and noun phrases) that function as direct objects, indirect objects, and objects of prepositions. The object pronouns are me, you, him, her, it, us, and them.

> They gave Susan the toy car for the children.
> They gave it to her for them.

B On a separate sheet of paper, rewrite the sentences, replacing the underlined nouns and noun phrases with pronouns.

> Matt didn't break the plate. *He didn't break it.*

1 Our children love TV.
2 Janet and I never buy food at that store.
3 Do you and I have the car this afternoon?
4 Sylvia's family laughs at her jokes.
5 My friends are speaking with Ms. Rowe today.

6 Mr. Harris is teaching the students with Mr. Cooper.
7 All the students are speaking English very well this year.
8 Does Carl need to give the paper to his teachers?
9 Martin and Larry returned the money to the woman.

TOP NOTCH 2B

Writing Booster

A subordinating conjunction connects a dependent clause to an independent clause.

——————— independent clause ———————   ——————— dependent clause ———————
People are eating more fast foods today   because they want to save time.
     I generally avoid carbohydrates   even though it isn't easy.

Subordinating conjunctions	
because	unless
since	although
if	(even) though

A dependent clause can also come at the beginning of a sentence. Use a comma after the dependent clause when it comes first.

——————— dependent clause ———————   ——————— independent clause ———————
Because people want to save time,   they are eating more fast foods today.
     Even though it isn't easy, I generally avoid carbohydrates.

Use the subordinating conjunction <u>if</u> to express a condition. Use <u>unless</u> to express a negative condition.
   You will be healthy if you eat right and exercise regularly.
   You will gain weight unless you eat right and exercise regularly. (= if you don't)

Use the subordinating conjunctions <u>although</u>, <u>even though</u>, or <u>though</u> to express a contradiction.
Although
Even though   they knew fatty foods were unhealthy, people ate them anyway.
Though

Remember: Use <u>because</u> or <u>since</u> to give a reason.

A   Choose the best subordinating conjunction to complete each sentence.

1 (Though / If / Unless) I learn to speak English well, I will be very happy.

2 (Even though / Because / If) she is an artist, she is interested in science.

3 Studying English is important (although / because / unless) it can help you do more.

4 (Unless / Although / Since) English grammar isn't easy, I like studying it.

5 They have to go on a diet (because / unless / though) they're overweight.

6 He cut back on desserts and sodas (even though / if / because) he didn't want to.

7 (Even though / Because / Unless) my grandmother is 80 years old, she is in very good health.

8 (Unless / Because / Though) I think I'm going to get sick, I don't want to change my eating habits.

9 She won't eat red meat (because / unless / although) she has to.

10 (Unless / Even though / Since) she's a vegetarian, she sometimes eats fish.

B   Read each sentence. Then, on a separate sheet of paper, write and connect a clause to the sentence, using the subordinating conjunction.

1 Most people don't want to change their eating habits. (even though)

2 Children become overweight. (if)

3 Obesity will continue to be a global problem. (unless)

4 Eating too much fast food is bad for you. (because)

5 Most people continue to eat unhealthy foods. (although)

> *1 Most people don't want to change their eating*
> *habits even though they have health problems.*

C   Guidance for the Writing Exercise (on page 72) Using four different subordinating conjunctions, write four sentences: two about eating habits in the past and two about eating habits in the present. Use your sentences in your paragraph about eating habits.

When writing a series of words or phrases in a sentence, be sure that all items in the series are in the same grammatical form. This feature of good writing is called "parallel structure."

Lucy is creative. She likes painting, playing the piano, and dancing. (all items in the series are gerunds)

Be careful! Don't combine gerunds and infinitives in the same series.
Don't write: Lucy is creative. She likes painting, ~~to play~~ the piano, and dancing.

In a series of infinitives, it is correct to use <u>to</u> before each item in the series or to use <u>to</u> only before the first item.

✗ I decided to study medicine, get married, and ~~to~~ have children before my thirtieth birthday.
✓ I decided to study medicine, to get married, and to have children before my thirtieth birthday.
✓ I decided to study medicine, get married, and have children before my thirtieth birthday.

Remember: When a sentence includes a series of more than two words or phrases, separate them with commas. Use <u>and</u> before the last item in the series. The comma before <u>and</u> is optional.

no comma (two items)   commas (three items)
Jake and May have three favorite activities: painting, singing, and dancing.

A   Correct the errors in parallel structure in the sentences.

1   I have begun studying psychology and to learn about personality development.
2   They avoid arguing about the nature-nurture controversy and to disagree about which is more important.
3   The Bersons love to run, to swim, and lift weights.
4   She's both responsible and social. She prefers to study early in the evening and going out afterwards.
5   Introverts hate to talk about their feelings and being with a lot of people.
6   Marjorie is a classic extrovert. She likes to be very active, knowing a lot of people, and to seek excitement.
7   To be quiet, be hard to know, and to seek peace are traits typical of the introvert's personality.
8   Psychologists of the nineteenth century continued believing in the importance of genetics and to write about it in books and articles.

B   Guidance for the Writing Exercise (on page 84)   On a separate sheet of paper, write sentences to answer some or all the following questions about the person you chose. If appropriate, use verbs and phrases from the box on the right. Be careful to use parallel structure. Use the sentences in your paragraphs about the person.

- Who is the person?
- What is his or her relation to you?
- Who are the people in his or her family?
- How many siblings does he or she have?
- What kind of personality does he or she have?
- What are his or her likes and dislikes?
- Are there some things he or she is excited about, bored with, angry about, or worried about right now?
- Are there some things he or she is excited about, bored with, angry about, or worried about right now?

Words to describe likes / dislikes	
avoids	hopes
hates	would like
can't stand	is happy about
doesn't mind	is excited about
enjoys	is bored with
expects	is sick and tired of

Remember: A good paragraph has a topic sentence that clearly states what the main idea of the paragraph is.

In addition, a paragraph should have **supporting details**—that is, information that provides support for, and is clearly tied to, the topic sentence.

Be careful! If a detail doesn't support the topic sentence or isn't tied to it clearly, then it may not belong in the paragraph.

In the writing model to the right, the topic sentence of the paragraph is highlighted in yellow. The sentences that follow are details. Two of the sentences are crossed out because they do not support the topic sentence and should not be included in the paragraph. These two sentences do not provide information about the chair and do not indicate why the writer likes the chair. The remaining sentences are supporting details—they all support the topic sentence and are clearly tied to it. They provide more information about the chair and they explain why the writer likes the chair.

In my living room, my favorite possession is an old wooden chair. My parents gave it to me when I left home. A wooden chair can be very expensive if it is an antique. It has lots of memories for me because it was in my parents' bedroom when I was growing up. It's important to take very good care of wooden furniture. The chair is very comfortable, and I used to sit in it a lot as a child.

A Read each topic sentence. Circle the detail that does not support the topic sentence.

1 Many French artists in the nineteenth century were influenced by Japanese art and printmaking.
   a Today, the work of Hokusai, Japan's most famous printmaker, is popular in Western countries.
   b Looking at the work of the French impressionists, it is clear that they chose to imitate the Japanese artistic styles of the time.
   c A number of French artists had collections of Japanese art.

2 I love my poster of Álvaro Saborío, the Costa Rican soccer player, but my wife hates it.
   a I think Saborío is a great player.
   b My wife doesn't think I should keep it in our bedroom.
   c The number on Saborío's uniform is 15.

3 Rodin's statue, *The Thinker*, is probably one of the most famous sculptures in the world.
   a This metal sculpture of a man deep in thought is recognized all over the world.
   b Rodin was born on November 12, 1840.
   c The image of *The Thinker* can be seen in popular art and advertisements.

4 On a side table in my dining room, I have two small ceramic figures of lions from my trip to Taipei.
   a They have beautiful colors including red, green, blue, and yellow.
   b You should visit the National Palace Museum when you are in Taipei.
   c I bought them together from a small shop at a temple I was visiting.

5 My sister has always shown a lot of talent in the performing arts.
   a We've had our differences, and we haven't always agreed on everything.
   b She has acted in school plays since she was about ten years old.
   c I think she's going to follow a career as an actor or dancer.

6 I think artistic talent is something you're born with.
   a I've tried many times to improve my ability at drawing, but it hasn't worked.
   b I have friends who are very talented in art, but they've never taken any special classes.
   c My aunt studied art at the Art Institute of Chicago for four years.

B   Guidance for the Writing Exercise (on page 96) On the notepad, write the favorite object you chose.
Create a topic sentence that states the most important thing you want to say about that object.
Then write five supporting details to use in your paragraph.

Favorite object:
Topic sentence:
Details to support my topic sentence:
1.
2.
3.
4.
5.

UNIT 9   Organizing ideas

When you want to describe the benefits and problems of an issue, there are different ways you can organize your ideas.
Here are some approaches.

Approach 1: In one paragraph

One way is to describe all the advantages and disadvantages in one paragraph. Following are notes of the details that
will be included in the paragraph.

THE ADVANTAGES AND DISADVANTAGES OF SMART PHONES
Advantages: are easy to carry, don't miss calls, keep you connected with family and friends
Disadvantages: bother other people, make people dependent, are easy to lose

This approach is good for a short piece of writing consisting of only a few sentences. However, if you want to develop
those ideas in more than just a few sentences, it is easier for the reader to follow if you can organize the details in one
of the following ways:

Approach 2: In two paragraphs

In this approach, you can use a first paragraph to describe all the advantages. Then you can use a second paragraph to
describe all the disadvantages. Following are notes of the details that will be included in each paragraph.

Paragraph 1: SMART PHONES HAVE ADVANTAGES
are easy to carry, don't miss calls, keep you connected with family and friends
Paragraph 2: BUT THEY ALSO HAVE DISADVANTAGES
bother other people, make people dependent, are easy to lose

Approach 3: In more than two paragraphs

In this approach, you can use a separate paragraph to focus on each different topic. In each paragraph, you can
describe both advantages and disadvantages. Following are notes of the details that will be included in each paragraph.

Paragraph 1: (THEY'RE SMALL.) smart phones easy to carry, but also easy to lose
Paragraph 2: (THEY'RE CONVENIENT.) won't miss calls, but you can also bother other people
Paragraph 3: (THEY'VE CHANGED OUR LIVES.) keep people connected with family and friends, but also
can make people dependent

A Using Approach 2, organize the ideas into two paragraphs: paragraph 1 is about the benefits of renting a car; paragraph 2 is about the problems. Write 1 or 2 next to each idea.

____ It gives you the freedom to go wherever you want to go whenever you want.

____ You might see places you can't see by bus or train.

____ You could have an accident during your trip.

____ You have more control over whether or not you will have an accident during your trip.

____ You can carry more luggage and other things you might need.

____ To drive safely, you have to become familiar with the local driving rules.

____ If you're traveling with a group of people, it could cost less than paying for bus and train tickets.

____ You may have to understand road signs that are in a different language.

____ If you have to do all the driving, it can be very stressful and tiring.

____ If you're traveling alone or with one other person, it could cost a lot of money in rental fees and gas.

B Now, on a separate sheet of paper, practice using Approach 3. Organize the sentences from Exercise A by topic into three or more separate paragraphs. Don't forget to include a topic sentence.

C Guidance for the Writing Exercise (on page 108) Use your notes on page 107 to write your paragraphs about the benefits and problems of the Internet. Choose Approach 2 or Approach 3 to organize your writing.

UNIT 10 Introducing conflicting ideas: On the one hand; On the other hand

Use <u>On the one hand</u> and <u>On the other hand</u> to present conflicting ideas or two sides of an issue. The following two sentences present the two sides together, one right after the other.

On the one hand, I would want to tell the truth. On the other hand, I wouldn't want to get in trouble.

Remember: You can also present conflicting or contradictory information with <u>Even though</u>, <u>Although</u>, and <u>However</u>.

Even though I'm basically an honest person, I don't always tell the truth.

Although Matt didn't think he broke the dish, it's possible that he did.

Matt wanted to tell the owner of the store what happened. However, Noah didn't agree.

When one paragraph presents one side of an issue and the next one presents the other, writers don't usually use <u>On the one hand</u> in the first paragraph. Instead, they just begin the next paragraph with <u>On the other hand</u> to let the reader know that the conflicting idea will follow. Look at the writing model to the right.

Being honest has many advantages. If you always tell the truth, you don't have to remember an untruth you said before. People who tell the truth don't have trouble sleeping. They can look at themselves in the mirror and feel good.

On the other hand, there are times when telling a lie makes sense. For example, your friend Andrew might ask you if you like his new jacket, and you think it's ugly. If you told him that, it would hurt his feelings. It's possible that not being absolutely truthful might make more sense.

A Reread the Photo Story on page 111. Write a summary of the story in three to five sentences. Answer the questions below.

- Where was Matt?
- Who was he with?
- What happened?
- What did the two friends discuss?

B Answer the questions below. Write three to five sentences about Matt's choices. Then write the consequences of each choice. Use <u>If</u> and the unreal conditional in at least one sentence.

- What should he do?
- What could he do?
- What would most people do?

C Write three to five sentences about what you would do if you were Matt. Answer the questions below.

- What would you do?
- What would happen if you did that?
- What would happen if you didn't?

D Guidance for the Writing Exercise (on page 120) In your paragraphs about Matt's dilemma, use <u>On the one hand</u>, <u>On the other hand</u>, <u>Even though</u>, <u>Although</u>, and <u>However</u> to connect conflicting ideas.

Top Notch Pop Lyrics

▶ 1:16–1:17 **Greetings and Small Talk**
[Unit 1]

You look so familiar. Have we met before?
I don't think you're from around here.
It might have been two weeks ago, but I'm not sure.
Has it been a month or a year?
I have a funny feeling that I've met you twice.
That's what they call déjà vu.
You were saying something friendly, trying to be nice—and now you're being friendly, too.
One look, one word.
It's the friendliest sound that I've ever heard.
Thanks for your greetings.
I'm glad this meeting occurred.

(CHORUS)
**Greetings and small talk
make the world go round.
On every winding road I've walked,
this is what I've found.**

Have you written any letters to your friends back home?
Have you had a chance to do that?
Have you spoken to your family on the telephone?
Have you taken time for a chat?
Bow down, shake hands.
Do whatever you do in your native land.
I'll be happy to greet you
in any way that you understand.

(CHORUS)

Have you seen the latest movie out of Hollywood?
Have you read about it yet?
If you haven't eaten dinner, are you in the mood for a meal you won't forget?
Bow down, shake hands.
Do whatever you do in your native land.
I'll be happy to greet you
in any way that you understand.

(CHORUS)

▶ 1:35–1:36 **Better Late Than Never**
[Unit 2]

Where have you been? I've waited for you.
I'd rather not say how long.
The movie began one hour ago.
How did you get the time all wrong?
Well, I got stuck in traffic, and when I arrived
I couldn't find a parking place.
Did you buy the tickets? You're kidding—
for real?
Let me pay you back, in that case.

(CHORUS)
**Sorry I'm late.
I know you've waited here forever.
How long has it been?
It's always better late than never.**

When that kind of movie comes to the big screen,
it always attracts a crowd,
and I've always wanted to see it with you—
but it looks like we've missed it now.
I know what you're saying, but actually,
I would rather watch a video.

So why don't we rent it and bring it back home?
Let's get in the car and go.

(CHORUS)

Didn't you mention, when we made our plans, that you've seen this movie recently?
It sounds so dramatic, and I'm so upset,
I'd rather see a comedy!
Well, which comedy do you recommend?
It really doesn't matter to me.
I still haven't seen 'The World and a Day'.
I've heard that one is pretty funny.

(CHORUS)

▶ 2:17–2:18 **Checking Out**   [Unit 3]

Ms. Jones travels all alone.
She doesn't need much space—
a single room with a nice twin bed
and a place for her suitcase.
Her stay is always satisfactory,
but in the morning she's going to be checking out.
Mr. Moon will be leaving soon,
and when he does I'll say,
"Thank you, sir, for staying with us.
How do you want to pay?"
And in the end it isn't hard.
He'll put it on his credit card. He's checking out.
Would you like to leave a message?
Could you call back later?
Do you need some extra towels
or today's newspaper?
Can I get you anything?
Would you like room service?
I'm so sorry.
Am I making you nervous?
Good evening.
I'll ring that room for you.
Is that all?
I'll be glad to put you through.
I'm sorry, but he's not answering.
The phone just rings and rings.
The couple in room 586
have made a king-size mess.
Pick up the laundry. Turn down the beds.
We have another guest
coming with his family.
You'd better hurry or they will be checking out. . .

▶ 2:36–2:37 **Wheels around the World**   [Unit 4]

Was I going too fast
or a little too slow?
I was looking out the window,
and I just don't know.
I must have turned the steering wheel
a little too far
when I drove into the bumper
of that luxury car.
Oh no!
How awful!
What a terrible day!
I'm sorry to hear that.
Are you OK?

(CHORUS)
**Wheels around the World
are waiting here with your car.
Pick it up.
Turn it on.
Play the radio.
Wheels around the World—
"helping you to go far."
You can drive anywhere.
Buckle up and go.**

Did I hit the red sedan,
or did it hit me?
I was talking on the cell phone
in my SUV.
Nothing was broken,
and no one was hurt,
but I did spill some coffee
on my favorite shirt.
Oh no!
Thank goodness you're still alive!
I'm so happy that
you survived.

(CHORUS)

What were you doing when you hit that tree?
I was racing down the mountain, and the brakes failed me.
How did it happen? Was the road still wet?
Well, there might have been a danger sign,
But I forget.
The hood popped open and the door fell off.
The headlights blinked and the
engine coughed.
The side-view mirror had a terrible crack.
The gearshift broke. Can I bring the
car back?
Oh no!
Thank goodness
you're still alive!
I'm so happy that
you survived.

(CHORUS)

▶ 3:17–3:18 **Piece of Cake**   [Unit 5]

I need to pick up a few things
on the way back to school.
Feel like stopping at a store with me?
I'd like to, but I think I'll pass.
I don't have time today.
It's already nearly a quarter to three.

(CHORUS)
**Don't worry. We'll be fine.
How long can it take?
It's easy. It'll be a piece of cake.**

I need a tube of toothpaste and
a bar of Luvly soap,
some sunscreen, and a bottle of shampoo.
Where would I find makeup?
How about a comb?
Have a look in aisle one or two.

(CHORUS)

I have an appointment
for a haircut at The Spa.
On second thought, they're always
running late.
My class starts in an hour.
I'll never make it now.
How long do you think we'll have to wait?

(CHORUS)
They say there's someone waiting
for a trim ahead of me.
Can I get you some coffee or some tea?
OK. In the meantime,
I'll be getting something strong
for this headache at the pharmacy!

(CHORUS)

▶ 3:37–3:38 **A Perfect Dish** [Unit 6]
I used to eat a lot of fatty foods,
but now I just avoid them.
I used to like chocolate and lots of sweets,
but now those days are gone.
To tell you the truth,
it was too much trouble.
They say you only live once,
but I'm not crazy about feeling sick.
What was going wrong?
Now I know I couldn't live without this.
Everything's ready.
Why don't you sit down?

(CHORUS)
It looks terrific,
but it smells pretty awful.
What in the world can it be?
It smells like chicken,
and it tastes like fish—
a terrific dish
for you and me—
a perfect dish for you
and me.

I used to be a big meat eater,
now I'm vegetarian,
and I'm not much of a coffee drinker.
I can't stand it anymore.
I'm avoiding desserts with sugar.
I'm trying to lose some weight.
Some things just don't agree with me.
They're bad for me, I'm sure.
Would you like some?
Help yourself.
Isn't it so good for you health?

(CHORUS)
Aren't you going to have some?
Don't you like it?
Wasn't it delicious?
Don't you want some more?

(CHORUS)

▶ 4:13–4:14 **The Colors of Love** [Unit 7]
Are you sick and tired of working hard day
and night?
Do you like to look at the world in shades of
black and white?
Your life can still be everything that you were
dreaming of.
Just take a look around you and see all the
colors of love.
You wake up every morning and go through
the same old grind.
You don't know how the light at the window
could be so unkind. If blue is the color that
you choose when the road is rough, you know
you really need to believe in the colors of love.

(CHORUS)
The colors of love
are as beautiful as a rainbow.

The colors of love
shine on everyone in the world.
Are negative thoughts and emotions painful
to express?
They're just tiny drops in the ocean of
happiness.
And these are the feelings you must learn to
rise above.
Your whole life is a picture you paint with the
colors of love.

(CHORUS)

▶ 4:28–4:29 **To Each His Own** [Unit 8]
He doesn't care for Dali.
The colors are too bright.
He says that Picasso
got everything just right.
She can't stand the movies
that are filmed in Hollywood.
She likes Almodóvar.
She thinks he's really good.
He's inspired by everything
she thinks is second-rate.
She's moved and fascinated
by the things he loves to hate.
He's crazy about art that only
turns her heart to stone.
I guess that's why they say
to each his own.
He likes pencil drawings.
She prefers photographs.
He takes her to the the art museum,
but she just laughs and laughs.
He loves the Da Vinci
that's hanging by the door.
She prefers the modern art
that's lying on the floor.
"No kidding! You'll love it. Just wait and see.
It's perfect in every way."
She shakes her head. "It's not for me.
It's much too old and gray."
She thinks he has the worst taste
that the world has ever known.
I guess that's why they say
to each his own.
But when it's time to say goodbye,
they both feel so alone.
I guess that's why they say
to each his own.

▶ 5:16–5:17 **Life in Cyberspace** [Unit 9]
I'm just fooling around.
Am I interrupting you?
Well, I wanted to know—
what are you up to?
I tried to send some photos,
but it's been so long
that I almost don't remember
how to log on.
So I'm thinking about getting a
new computer.
I don't know what kind. I should have done
it sooner.
But I heard the Panatel is as good as
the rest.
Check it out. Check it out.
You should really check it out.

(CHORUS)
Let's face it—that's life.
That's life in cyberspace.

When you download the pictures,
then you open the files.
If your computer's slow,
then it can take a little while.
From the pull-down menu,
you can print them, too.
But don't forget to save
everything you do.
Scroll it up. Scroll it down.
Put your cursor on the bar.
Then click on the icon,
and you'll see my new car!
The car goes as fast
as the one I had before.
Check it out. Check it out.
You should really check it out.

(CHORUS)
Am I talking to myself, or are you still there?
This instant message conversation's
going nowhere.
I could talk to Liz.
She isn't nearly as nice.
It isn't quite as much fun.
I've done it once or twice.
What's the problem?
Come on. Give it a try.
If you don't want to be friends,
at least tell me why.
Did you leave to make a call
or go out to get some cash?
Did the photos I sent make your
computer crash?

(CHORUS)

▶ 5:31–5:32 **What Would You Do?**
[Unit 10]
What would you do
if I got a tattoo with your name?
What would you say
if I dyed my hair for you?
What would you do
if I sang outside your window?
What would you think
if I told you I loved you?

(CHORUS)
I hate to say this,
but I think you're making a big mistake.
By tomorrow,
I'm sure you'll be sorry.

What would you do
if I sent you a love letter?
Would you say it was wrong
and send it back to me?
What would you think
if I pierced my ears? Would you care?
Would you think
that I had lost all my modesty?

(CHORUS)
Well, give it some thought.
I know I could make you happy.
Are you kidding?
You'd have to be nuts to ask me.
It's no mistake. I'm sure
that my heart is yours.
I have to find a way
to make you mine.

(CHORUS)

THIRD EDITION

TOP NOTCH 2B

WORKBOOK

JOAN SASLOW
ALLEN ASCHER

with Terra Brockman and Julie C. Rouse

1 Look at the Healthy Diet Plate. Then read the statements. Check <u>true</u> or <u>false</u>.

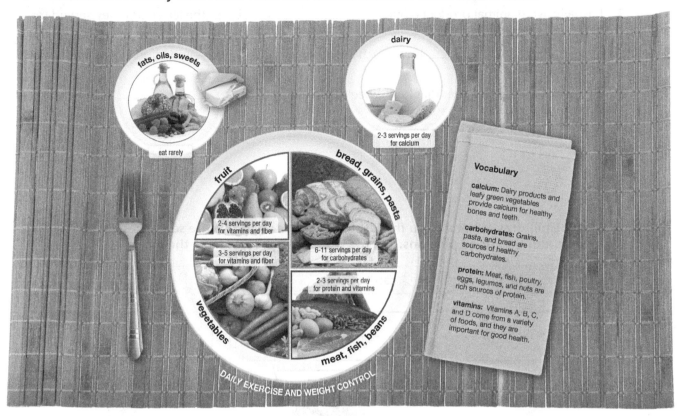

	true	false
1. You should eat 3 servings per day of carbohydrates.	☐	☐
2. You should eat more vegetables than fruit.	☐	☐
3. You should avoid breads and grains.	☐	☐
4. Dairy products are a good source of fiber.	☐	☐
5. You should eat fruit for carbohydrates.	☐	☐
6. Exercise is an important part of a healthy life.	☐	☐

2 Rewrite the false statements in Exercise 1 to make them true.

3 Complete the statements with phrases from the box.

I'd better pass	I have no idea	I'm watching my weight
I have to admit	I couldn't resist	

1. I'm on a low-fat diet because _____.

2. The pasta looks delicious, but _____. I'm on the Atkins diet.

3. I usually avoid animal products, but _____ the ice cream they served for dessert. I just had to have it!

4. _____ how much fat is in this cheeseburger—and I don't want to know. I just want to enjoy it!

5. Eating a low-fat, high-fiber diet hasn't been easy, but _____ I look and feel better as a result.

4 Look at the pictures. What do you think the people are saying? Write sentences about the people and their food passions. Use the words and phrases from the box.

addict	big ____ eater	can't stand	crazy about	don't care for	love

1. I'm crazy about asparagus.

2. _____

3. _____

4. _____

5. _____

6. _____

5 Read about Kate's food passions. Then complete each sentence with <u>used to</u> or <u>didn't use to</u> and the verb.

When I was a kid, I loved sweets. I think I ate about five cookies a day! When I was a teenager, I started eating a lot of meat. I had steaks and fries almost every day. I didn't care for vegetables or fruit. Then on my 20ᵗʰ birthday, I decided I needed a change, so I became a vegetarian. These days I eat meat again, but I avoid fatty foods and sugar. I've lost a lot of weight and I feel much better.

Kate

1. Kate _____ a lot of sweets, but now she avoids sugar.
   eat

2. When she was a teenager, she _____ fatty foods.
   have

3. Before she turned 20, she _____ vegetables.
   like

4. She _____ a vegetarian, but now she eats meat.
   be

5. Kate _____ care of herself, but now she eats well.
   take

LESSON 2

6 Choose the correct response. Write the letter on the line.

1. _____ "Please help yourself."

2. _____ "I'll pass on the chocolates."

3. _____ "Don't you eat chicken?"

4. _____ "I'm sorry. I didn't know you were on a diet."

5. _____ "I'm a coffee addict. What about you?"

a. Actually, I've been cutting back.

b. Thanks. Everything smells so good.

c. It's not a problem.

d. Don't you eat sweets?

e. Actually, no. It's against my religion.

7 Complete the statements with a food or drink to describe your own food preferences.

1. I'm not crazy about _____.

2. I'm avoiding _____.

3. I don't care for _____.

4. I'm not much of a _____ drinker.

5. _____ doesn't / don't agree with me.

8 Complete the conversation with phrases from the box.

| is a vegetarian | is on a diet | is allergic to | doesn't care for | is avoiding |

A: Let's have a dinner party Friday night. Help me prepare the menu.

B: OK. Remember that my sister _____, so we can't make anything too fatty. Why don't you make some chicken?

A: I would, but Stella _____. She never eats meat. Maybe I can make that rice dish.

B: I don't know. Miguel is trying to eat healthy, whole-grain foods, so he _____ white rice these days.

A: OK . . . Then how about black bean soup with peppers?

B: Uh, I don't think Julio would like that. He _____ spicy food.

A: Is there anything that everyone can eat?

B: Hmm . . . I don't know, but I hope you'll make that delicious chocolate cake for dessert!

A: I can't. Don't you remember how sick Paul was at our last dinner? He _____ chocolate!

B: I've got an idea—why don't we just go out to eat? Then everyone can order what they want!

9 Complete each negative <u>yes</u> / <u>no</u> question.

1. **A:** _Didn't you go to Latvia_ last year?
   B: Yes, I did. I went to Latvia in August.

2. **A:** _____ meat?
   B: No, I don't. I never touch meat.

3. **A:** _____ a doctor?
   B: No, she's not. David's mother is a dentist.

4. **A:** _____ a great play?
   B: Yes, it was terrific.

5. **A:** _____ more noodles?
   B: No, thanks. I'm full. I've had enough.

6. **A:** _____ China before?
   B: Actually, no. But I've been to Korea.

LESSON 3

10 Read the article "How Can It Be?" on page 68 of the Student's Book again. Then complete the chart.

EXTRA READING COMPREHENSION

American eating habits	French eating habits
	consume rich foods, but stay thin
"clean their plates"	
	spend a long time at the table
drive to the supermarket	
	buy fresh food daily

11 Answer the questions with information from the article on page 68 of the Student's Book.

1. How do the French see eating? How do Americans see eating?

   _____

2. Why do Americans "keep eating long after the French would have stopped"?

   _____

3. What lifestyle change has affected French eating habits recently?

   _____

12 Read the online article about making lifestyle changes.

How to make healthy lifestyle changes that last

If you've ever tried to change the way you eat or to lead a more active lifestyle, you know it isn't easy. Making a lifestyle change is challenging and it's especially difficult to make changes that last. Often people try to make many big changes all at once without a clear idea of how they will accomplish their goals. They may struggle, get disappointed, and give up after a short period of time. Here are some tips to help you make healthy changes that become lifelong habits:

1 Make one change at a time. Replacing unhealthy behaviors with healthy ones takes time. If you try to change too much too fast, you won't be successful. Focus on one change you'd like to make. If your goal is to improve your eating habits, choose one thing to cut back on or add to your diet. Maybe resolve to stop drinking soda or eat some vegetables or fruit with every meal. When a new healthy behavior becomes part of your normal daily routine, you can take on another change.

2 Start small. Changes are often easier to make if they are small. Don't expect yourself to go from lying on the sofa watching TV every night to spending an hour a night at the gym. Instead, take "baby steps." For example, you could start by exercising twice a week for 30 minutes. Then, when you've done this successfully for a few weeks, try three times a week for 45 minutes.

3 Make a realistic plan. When you decide to make a lifestyle change, you need to plan what you will do and when, where, how often, etc. If more exercise is your goal, figure out how you will schedule it into your week and put it on your calendar. If you want to eat healthier, write down meals and snacks for the week. Keep the foods you'll need on hand, and consult your plan before you eat. Make sure the plan you create is achievable and that it works for your lifestyle. For example, if you're a big meat eater, a plan to eat only vegetables is not going to happen! Likewise, if you're not a morning person, don't plan daily workouts at 5:00 A.M.!

13 Complete the statements with words and phrases from the box.

"baby step"	challenging	habits	realistic	struggle	successful

1. You want the changes you make to become _____ which you do regularly without thinking.

2. It's difficult to make lifestyle changes. You may _____, but don't give up.

3. If you try to make many big changes all at once, you probably won't be _____.

4. If you want to stop drinking coffee, you could start by drinking two cups every morning instead of three. This is a _____.

5. When you plan to make a change, be _____. Set goals you can accomplish and that work for your lifestyle.

6. Trying to change the way you eat is _____. It takes a lot of effort.

14 Think about a lifestyle change you have tried to make. Was your change successful? On a separate sheet of paper, explain why or why not.

15 Complete the postcard with the correct form of <u>taste</u>, <u>smell</u>, or <u>look</u>.

Hi Reiko,

I'm having a great time in Marrakech! Yesterday I walked in the main square, and it _____ like a scene from a movie!
1.
People in long, beautiful robes were everywhere, and there was so much food! I saw some fish that _____ like the kind we have
2.
at home. Somewhere else in the market, I couldn't see where, there was a kind of grilled meat that _____ terrific. I found it, but didn't know if I should try it. It
3.
_____ kind of strange, but I bought some anyway. It was delicious! It
4.
_____ both spicy and sweet. It wasn't at all what I expected!
5.
You should come here on your next vacation!

See you soon,

Junko

16 Complete the word webs. Write three examples of foods that match each adjective.

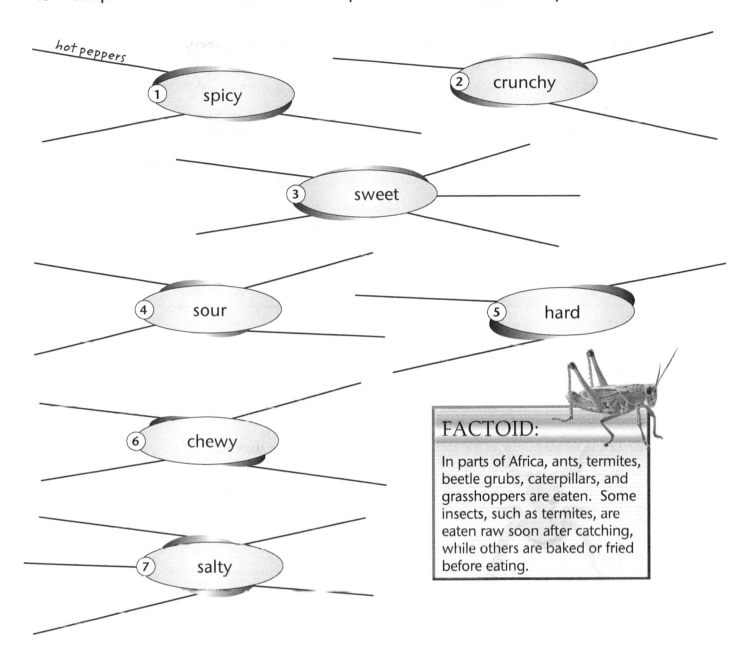

hot peppers

1 spicy

2 crunchy

3 sweet

4 sour

5 hard

6 chewy

7 salty

FACTOID:

In parts of Africa, ants, termites, beetle grubs, caterpillars, and grasshoppers are eaten. Some insects, such as termites, are eaten raw soon after catching, while others are baked or fried before eating.

17 Describe an unusual dish you have tried. Where and when did you eat it? What did it look, smell, and taste like? Would you recommend it to someone or not?

One of the strangest things I've ever eaten is . . .

A Read the statements. Then write a sentence with <u>use to</u> or <u>used to</u> about a habitual action that is no longer true today.

1. Since Charlie started going to the gym every day, he's lost so much weight.

   Charlie didn't use to go to the gym every day.

2. When he wasn't working, Scott made dinner every night. Now he doesn't have time.

   _____

3. Paul began getting up early every day when he had children.

   _____

4. As Cindy got older, her tastes changed. Now she actually likes vegetables.

   _____

5. I can't believe Judy doesn't eat meat anymore!

   _____

6. When Peter's doctor told him that he had better stop smoking, he quit.

   _____

7. After Pamela and Ed got married, they bought their first car.

   _____

B Write a <u>yes</u> / <u>no</u> question for each response, using a form of <u>used to</u>.

1. **A:** *Did you use to work in that part of the city?*

   B: Yes, I did. I used to work in that part of the city a few years ago.

2. **A:** _____

   B: No, they didn't. People didn't use to read the news online.

3. **A:** _____

   B: Yes, it did. Breakfast used to be free at the Windfield Inn.

4. **A:** _____

   B: No, they didn't. Foods didn't use to have labels.

5. **A:** _____

   B: Yes, I did. I used to live closer to work.

6. **A:** _____

   B: Yes, they did. Cars used to use a lot more gas.

7. **A:** _____

   B: No, I didn't. My brother used to drive a van, but not me.

C Complete the sentences with <u>be used to</u>, affirmative or negative.

1. Michelle has been on a low-fat, high-fiber diet for many years. She _____ fruits, vegetables, and whole grains. She _____ rich food, such as steak and ice cream.

2. Karen just got a haircut. It's very different from her old style. She _____ her new look yet.

3. We rented a minivan, but at home I drive a compact car. I _____ driving such a big car.

4. I _____ budget hotels, so it's a treat to stay in this expensive hotel with so many amenities.

5. Jeff is crazy about action movies. He _____ watching a lot of violence on the big screen.

D Complete the statements in your own way.

1. The Browns just moved from Alaska to Hawaii. They can't get used to _____
   _____.

2. Rose recently moved from a small town to a big city. She's getting used to _____
   _____.

3. Connor used to be a vegetarian. He still hasn't gotten used to _____.
   _____

Write three sentences about things you did often when you were a child. Use <u>would</u>.

When I was a child, I would play soccer all day on Saturdays.

1. _____
2. _____
3. _____

E Complete the conversations. Complete the negative <u>yes</u> / <u>no</u> questions and write short answers.

1. A: _____ you have any vegetarian friends?
   B: _____. None of my friends are vegetarian.

2. A: _____ you trying to lose weight?
   B: _____. I'm on a diet.

3. A: _____ he like spicy food?
   B: _____. He can't stand spicy food.

4. A: _____ there sardines on that pizza?
   B: _____. The pizza has sardines on it.

5. A: _____ Sandra allergic to fish?
   B: _____. She doesn't have any problem eating fish.

F Complete each conversation with a suggestion using <u>Why don't</u> or <u>Why doesn't.</u>

1. **A:** I'm too tired to cook dinner tonight.

   B: _____ go out to eat?

2. **A:** Mr. Lee's old van keeps breaking down.

   B: _____ buy a new car?

3. **A:** My mother thinks the hotel room will be too small.

   B: _____ reserve a suite?

4. **A:** That documentary was really long and boring!

   B: _____ watch a comedy next time?

WRITING BOOSTER

A Circle the best subordinating conjunction to complete each sentence.

1. It's important to eat fruits and vegetables (because / unless / although) they are sources of vitamins and fiber.

2. You should avoid fatty foods and sweets (unless / even though / if) you're watching your weight.

3. On the Atkins Diet, you can eat butter (since / even though / unless) it has a lot of fat.

4. You'll love the new Argentinean steakhouse El Matador—(unless / if / because) you're a vegetarian.

5. (If / Since / Though) Hannah doesn't care for fish or seafood, we didn't go out for sushi.

6. (Because / If / Although) she's cutting back on sweets, Danielle had a piece of cake at the birthday party.

7. Kate is avoiding dairy products (even though / unless / because) they don't agree with her.

8. (Unless / If / Since) he has to stay up late studying, Andrew doesn't drink coffee.

9. (Although / If / Unless) children are taught to always "clean their plates," they may become overweight.

10. (Unless / Though / Because) it's difficult to change your habits, you can succeed by making one small change at a time.

B Think about your eating habits today and your eating habits when you were younger. Write six sentences: three about your eating habits now and three about how you used to eat. Use subordinating conjunctions.

1. _____

2. _____

3. _____

4. _____

5. _____

6. _____

C On a separate sheet of paper, write a paragraph about how your eating habits have changed.

UNIT 7 About Personality

1 **Read each description. Then guess the color being described.**

1. People associate this color with power, intelligence, and sometimes evil. It's popular in fashion because it makes people look slimmer. _____

2. People associate this color with cleanliness and purity. It's popular in decorating because it goes with everything. _____

3. This is one of the most appealing colors. The color of the ocean and the sky, people find it peaceful and calming. It's a great color for a bedroom. It's not a good choice for a dining room—unless you're on a diet. _____

4. This color is associated with energy and excitement. It makes your heart beat faster—and increases your appetite. It's a popular color for fast cars and restaurants. In China, it means good luck. _____

2 **Read the Photo Story on page 75 of the Student's Book again. Match each phrase or statement with its meaning.**

1. _____ getting a little tired of   a. in my opinion it was

2. _____ to me it was   b. That's true. I hadn't thought of that.

3. _____ pulling your leg   c. I don't want to

4. _____ Good point.   d. looks good with all things

5. _____ I'd hate to have to   e. bored with

6. _____ on the wrong track   f. not thinking correctly about this

7. _____ goes with everything   g. joking by saying something that isn't true

3 **Write about your own color preferences.**

1. What's your favorite color? How does it make you feel?

   _____

2. What room in your home would you like to paint a different color? What color would you choose? Why?

   _____

3. Paint colors have names that describe specific shades—such as "tomato red" or "emerald green." Create a name for your favorite shade of your favorite color.

   _____

> **FACTOID: Men, women, and colors**
>
> **Studies have found that women prefer red over blue, but men prefer blue over red.**

4 Complete Lucia's letter. Use gerunds and infinitives. Remember to put the verbs in the correct tense.

Hi Rebecca,

   Well, I finally made a change! Last week I said to myself, "I _____ at our
                                                              1. can't stand / look
old kitchen walls one more day!" So I _____ them! My roommate Sara said
                                        2. decide / repaint
we should _____ a plan before we do it. She even _____
             3. discuss / make   4. suggest / take
a month or two to think about it. She said we should _____
                                                        5. practice / paint
first, but I already know how to paint. I don't _____. Anyway, I
                                                    6. need / learn
_____ new things. Finally, we _____ the kitchen a
   7. not mind / try   8. choose / give
cheerful color—bright yellow! I'm not sure, but Sara _____ the new
                                                        9. not seem / like
color. In fact, I don't think she _____! But I hope she does, because I
                                     10. enjoy / paint
_____ the living room next. I _____ it tomato red!
   11. plan / paint   12. would like / paint
What do you think about that?

Lucia

5 Complete each sentence with a gerund or infinitive and an adjective from the box.

annoying	boring	depressing	enjoyable	exciting	relaxing

1. I've had the most stressful week at work! I need _____ a massage this weekend.
                                                         get
   I find it so _____.

2. We don't want _____ tonight's game. Our favorite team is in the championship.
                     miss
   It's going to be really _____!

3. Most kids hate _____ shopping. They think it's not any fun and complain, "This is
                      go
   so _____."

4. I had to ask a classmate to please quit _____ his pencil on the desk. I found it very
                                              tap
   _____.

5. I don't feel like _____ that film. I hear it's very _____. I'm not in
                        watch
   the mood for a sad movie.

6. Max usually doesn't mind _____. He finds it pretty _____.
                               exercise

6 Write about your plans for the weekend. Use verbs with direct object infinitives, such as <u>need</u>, <u>plan</u>, <u>want</u>, and <u>would like</u>.

LESSON 2

7 Complete the conversation. Use the correct preposition with the verb or adjective, and a gerund.

A: You look a little blue. What's up?

B: Oh, nothing really. I'm just _____ sick of working _____ late every night.
        1. sick / work

A: Is that all? You look really down.

B: I'm _____ the same thing every day. And I also feel
        2. bored / do

   _____ too little time at home.
        3. sad / spend

A: Have you _____ overtime?
        4. complained / work

B: No. I'm _____ my boss angry. I had to _____ a report
        5. afraid / make   6. apologize / finish

   late. And now my boss is _____ us more work.
        7. talking / give

A: Wow! I see why you are feeling blue. Why don't you start looking for a new job?

B: Maybe I should.

FACTOID: Food to Improve Your Mood

Studies show that eating certain foods can help cheer you up when you are feeling blue. Eating foods that contain vitamins D and B and omega-3 fatty acids, such as fish, nuts, eggs, spinach, and bananas, increase the chemicals in your brain that make you feel happy and relaxed.

---

8 Suggest something to cheer the people up. Write complete sentences.

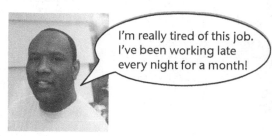

1. _____

_____

_____

2. _____

_____

_____

3. _____

_____

_____

4. _____

_____

_____

LESSON 3

9 Read the article about personality on page 80 of the Student's Book again. Then answer the questions.

1. What are people with easygoing personalities like? _____

_____

2. What type of personality is the opposite of easygoing? _____

_____

3. Why is it difficult to settle the "nature-nurture controversy"? _____

_____

4. Where do most experts believe our personalities come from? _____

_____

5. Do you think nature or nurture is more important in forming personality? Explain your answer.

_____

_____

10 Read the posts on an online message board. Rank the people from 1 to 5, with 1 being the least introverted and 5 being the most extroverted.

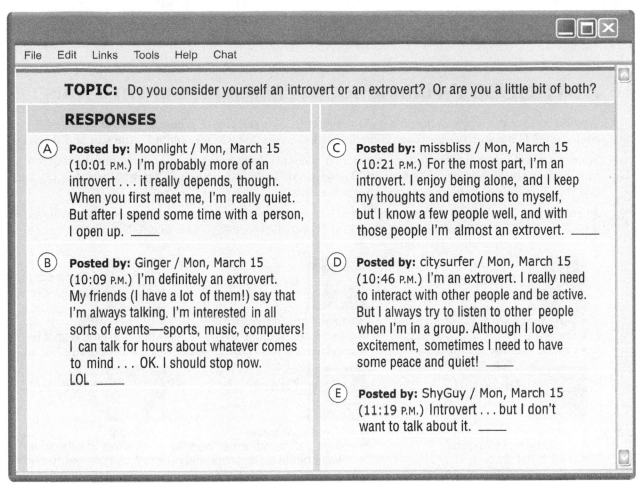

TOPIC: Do you consider yourself an introvert or an extrovert? Or are you a little bit of both?

RESPONSES

(A) **Posted by:** Moonlight / Mon, March 15 (10:01 P.M.) I'm probably more of an introvert . . . it really depends, though. When you first meet me, I'm really quiet. But after I spend some time with a person, I open up. ____

(B) **Posted by:** Ginger / Mon, March 15 (10:09 P.M.) I'm definitely an extrovert. My friends (I have a lot of them!) say that I'm always talking. I'm interested in all sorts of events—sports, music, computers! I can talk for hours about whatever comes to mind . . . OK. I should stop now. LOL ____

(C) **Posted by:** missbliss / Mon, March 15 (10:21 P.M.) For the most part, I'm an introvert. I enjoy being alone, and I keep my thoughts and emotions to myself, but I know a few people well, and with those people I'm almost an extrovert. ____

(D) **Posted by:** citysurfer / Mon, March 15 (10:46 P.M.) I'm an extrovert. I really need to interact with other people and be active. But I always try to listen to other people when I'm in a group. Although I love excitement, sometimes I need to have some peace and quiet! ____

(E) **Posted by:** ShyGuy / Mon, March 15 (11:19 P.M.) Introvert . . . but I don't want to talk about it. ____

11 Are you an introvert, an extrovert, or a little of both? Write your own reply to the message board topic in Exercise 10.

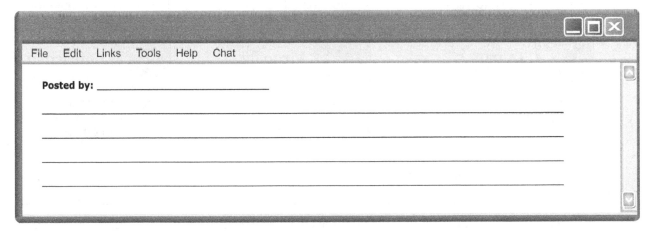

Posted by: _____

_____

_____

_____

_____

12   **Read the article about astrology. Then answer the questions.**

ASTROLOGY-FINDING YOUR PERSONALITY IN THE STARS

Why do you act the way you do? What is the secret to your emotions? Where does your personality come from? Is it nature or nurture? Genetics or the environment? Or could it be the sun and the stars?

Some people think that birth order influences personality, but many others believe that the day you were born on influences your personality. These people believe in astrology. They believe that the sun and the stars influence human personality and events.

Astrology may be a way to understand human personality. Or it may be a false science. But millions of people around the world read their astrological horoscope every day—just in case!

 Aquarius ♒
Jan 20–Feb 18
- very active
- cheerful
- can be a clown

 Gemini ♊
May 21–Jun 21
- worries about things
- can be self-critical
- can be hard to know

 Libra ♎
Sept 23–Oct 23
- conservative
- spends time with a few friends
- has strong emotions

 Pisces ♓
Feb 19–Mar 20
- honest
- easily bored with jobs
- likes quiet time

 Cancer ♋
Jun 22–Jul 22
- interested in travel
- enjoys being with other people
- always behaves appropriately

 Scorpio ♏
Oct 24–Nov 21
- friendly
- sensitive to others' emotions
- not easy to get to know

 Aries ♈
Mar 21–Apr 19
- enjoys being alone
- hard to get to know
- keeps thoughts and emotions inside

 Leo ♌
Jul 23–Aug 22
- happy with lots of people
- cheers people up
- crazy about nature

 Sagittarius ♐
Nov 22–Dec 21
- creative
- likes everything in moderation
- gets along with everyone

 Taurus ♉
Apr 20–May 20
- calm
- seeks peace
- good listener

 Virgo ♍
Aug 23–Sept 22
- keeps ideas inside
- likes to spend time alone
- enjoys reading

 Capricorn ♑
Dec 22–Jan 19
- has a lot of friends
- interested in events
- loves excitement

1.   What is the basic idea behind astrology? _____

_____

2.   Which of the zodiac signs describe more of an introvert? _____

3.   Which signs describe more of an extrovert? _____

4.   What zodiac sign are you? _____ Does the description for your sign describe

you? Why or why not? _____

_____

5. Compare the personality traits for your birth order with the personality traits for your zodiac sign. Are there any similarities? Which describes you better?

_____

_____

_____

GRAMMAR BOOSTER

A Complete each sentence with a gerund or an infinitive. Use verbs from the box. If either a gerund or an infinitive is correct, write both forms.

cook	do	drink	play	ride	study	watch

1. Susan can't stand _____ the dishes after dinner.

2. Michael loves _____ the guitar.

3. Marianna hates _____ for exams.

4. Joseph would like _____ his bike.

5. Beth doesn't mind _____ for her family.

6. Jim likes _____ TV.

7. My friend Jane avoids _____ whole milk.

B Unscramble the words and phrases to complete the conversations. Use a gerund or an infinitive.

1. A: John _can't stand thinking about graduation_____.
　　　　　think / about / can't stand / graduation

B: I know. _____.
　　　　　He / leave / hates / his friends

2. A: _____.
　　　　　refuse / dinner / tonight / I / make

B: Fine by me. _____.
　　　　　don't mind / go / I / out to eat

3. A: _____?
　　　　　buy / discussed / Have / you and Peter / a house

B: Yes. _____.
　　　　　find / We / would like / something bigger

4. A: _____.
　　　　　tonight / you / I / see / didn't expect

B: Well, _____.
　　　　　at the last minute / I / decided / come

C Complete each sentence. Circle the letter.

1. I love _____ TV in the evening.
   a. watch   **b.** to watch   **c.** watched

2. I hurt my knee last month, so I quit _____.
   a. jog   **b.** to jog   **c.** jogging

3. _____ too many sweets is bad for you.
   a. Eating   **b.** Eat   **c.** Eaten

4. My favorite thing to do after work is _____ magazines.
   a. read   **b.** to reading   **c.** to read

5. If you get an early start, you'll have a better chance of _____ your work on time.
   a. finish   **b.** finishing   **c.** to finish

6. I don't mind _____ the window. It's freezing in here!
   a. closing   **b.** close   **c.** closed

7. _____ opera well is a hard thing to do.
   a. Sing   **b.** To sing   **c.** To singing

D Find and correct seven errors in the diary.

> Usually I don't mind studying, but last night I was so sick of do homework that I decided to go out with Amy. She felt like go to the movies. I suggested a new romantic comedy that I'm excited about to see. But Amy said she can't stand romantic movies and suggested to watch an action movie instead. To me, watch violence is not appealing. So, finally, we agreed trying an animated film from Japan. We both found it really enjoyable. We're planning rent some other anime films to watch this weekend.

E Complete each sentence with an affirmative or negative gerund.

1. You should start _____ every day if you want to lose weight.
   exercise

2. Sue was worried about _____ enough money to pay her bills.
   have

3. When will you finish _____ on that project?
   work

4. Avoid _____ a cell phone while you're driving.
   use

5. Stella and I have considered _____ a new car. We just don't have the money.
   buy

6. I apologize for _____ you that I'd be late. I'm sorry that you've waited so long.
   tell

7. Let's start _____. I'm going to love _____ at that old wallpaper anymore!
   paint   *look*

8. Natalie has been working very long hours lately. She's depressed about _____ much time with her family.
   spend

9. I suggest _____ fatty foods. You'll be healthier.
   eat

A Complete each sentence. Circle the letter. Be careful to use parallel structure. One item has two correct answers.

1. Robert has begun to exercise, eat a healthy diet, and _____ plenty of sleep.
   a. getting   **b.** to get   **c.** get

2. Julia hates working long hours and _____ enough time with her family.
   a. not spending   **b.** to not spend   **c.** not spend

3. Virgos like to read and _____ time alone.
   a. spending   **b.** to spend   **c.** spend

4. Although he has been seeing a psychologist, he continues to feel down, to avoid interaction with others, and _____ all the time.
   a. feeling tired   **b.** to feel tired   **c.** feel tired

5. Enjoying being alone, being hard to get to know, and _____ and emotions inside are traits typical of an Aries.
   a. keeping thoughts   **b.** to keep thoughts   **c.** keep thoughts

6. Some typical behaviors of a middle child are to break rules, have a lot of friends, and _____ rebellious.
   a. being   **b.** to be   **c.** be

B Answer the questions about your own likes, dislikes, and personality. Answer in complete sentences, using words and phrases from Unit 7. Be careful to use parallel structure.

1. What are your likes? _____

_____

2. What are your dislikes? _____

_____

3. Which extrovert personality traits do you have? _____

_____

4. Which introvert personality traits do you have? _____

_____

5. What is your birth position in your family? _____

6. Which traits for this position describe you? _____

_____

7. What is your zodiac sign? _____

8. Which traits for this sign describe you? _____

_____

C On a separate sheet of paper, write at least two paragraphs about your personality. In the first paragraph, tell something about yourself. In the second paragraph, discuss where you think your personality traits come from—nature, nurture, birth order, and / or astrology.

1 Look at the paintings and read the conversation. Then read the statements and check <u>true</u> or <u>false</u>.

A Quiet Night by Charlotte Greene

Henry by Min Kyung Paek

Sophie: Is this painting by Charlotte Greene? I had no idea she had so much talent!

Gerald: She doesn't really look like the artistic type, does she?

Sophie: I guess you can't always judge a book by its cover. It's really quite good. What do you think?

Gerald: I find it a little weird, actually. It makes me feel nervous.

Sophie: But that's what makes it interesting. In my opinion, it's exciting.

Gerald: Hey, this is an interesting piece. It's by Min Kyung Paek. I love her work.

Sophie: I think it's kind of depressing.

Gerald: You do? Maybe you're just feeling a little blue today.

Sophie: No, I mean it. I guess I'm just not really into all the dark colors.

Gerald: Well, to each his own, I guess.

	true	false
1. Gerald is really into Charlotte Greene's painting.	☐	☐
2. Sophie likes Greene.	☐	☐
3. Gerald is a fan of Min Kyung Paek's art.	☐	☐
4. Sophie finds Paek's painting depressing.	☐	☐
5. Sophie prefers darker colors to brighter colors.	☐	☐
6. Sophie and Gerald like the same kind of art.	☐	☐

2 Write a plus (+) next to the statements that indicate that the person likes the art, and a minus (-) next to the statements that indicate that the person doesn't like it.

1. _____ I had no idea he had so much talent.
2. _____ Her work is very impressive.
3. _____ This abstract sculpture is fascinating.
4. _____ It's an unforgettable photograph.
5. _____ I find it a little boring, actually.

6. _____ I guess I'm just not really into modern art.
7. _____ It's a little weird, but that's what makes it so interesting.
8. _____ This is an unusual piece, but I don't find it appealing.

3 What do Sophie and Gerald think of the paintings on page 64? Complete the chart.

	Greene	Paek
Sophie's opinion		
Gerald's opinion		

4 CHALLENGE. Which painting in Exercise 1 do you prefer? Why? Write a few sentences expressing your opinion.

LESSON 1

5 Read each sentence and decide if it is in the active voice (A) or passive voice (P).

1. _____ Many people visit the Metropolitan Museum of Art in New York.
2. _____ The glass pyramid in front of the Louvre was finished in 1989.
3. _____ A color poster of the painting was made available.
4. _____ The museum catalog has been translated into many languages.
5. _____ Akira Kurosawa directed the film *Seven Samurai* in 1954.
6. _____ That vase was made in ancient Egypt.
7. _____ The photograph was taken fifty years ago.
8. _____ Matisse painted *La Musique* in 1910.

6 Use the information in the chart to write two sentences, one in the active voice and one in the passive voice. Be sure to use the correct verb with the artwork.

Art Object	Artist	Year
1. *Still Life with Watermelon* (painting)	Pablo Picasso	1946
2. *Vines and Olive Trees* (painting)	Joan Miró	1919
3. *The Raven and the First Men* (wood figure)	Bill Reid	1994
4. *Citizen Kane* (film)	Orson Welles	1941
5. *Waterfront Demonstration* (photograph)	Dorothea Lange	1934

1. Active: *Pablo Picasso painted Still Life with Watermelon in 1946.*

   Passive: *Still Life with Watermelon was painted by Pablo Picasso in 1946.*

2. Active: _____

   Passive: _____

3. Active: _____

   Passive: _____

4. Active: _____

   Passive: _____

5. Active: _____

   Passive: _____

7 Read a page from a tour guide about Paris. Complete the conversation. Make a recommendation to someone who is visiting Paris, using the information in the tour guide.

The Rodin Museum

There are many wonderful museums to see while you are visiting Paris. One museum you should be sure to visit is the lovely Rodin Museum. The Rodin Museum houses over 6,600 sculptures. There is also an impressive garden. A large number of sculptures are presented in this setting, including Rodin's most famous work, *The Thinker*. In addition to the sculptures, take a look at the excellent drawing collection. Many of Rodin's sketches are there.

YOU: Be sure _____
                                    1.
in Paris.

B: Really? Why's that?

YOU: Well, _____ .
                                    2.

B: No kidding!

YOU: They also _____
                                    3.
_____ .

You'll _____ .
                                    4.

B: Thanks for the recommendation.

8 Choose the correct response. Write the letter on the line.

1. _____ "Is this vase handmade?"
2. _____ "What do you think of this painting?"
3. _____ "Where was the figure made?"
4. _____ "Do you know when this photograph was taken?"
5. _____ "What's the bowl made of?"

a. Clay. It's handmade.
b. Yes, it is.
c. It says it was made in Bulgaria.
d. Not much. I'm not crazy about the colors.
e. Around 1980, I think.

9 Unscramble the words to write questions.

1. were / Where / built / those / wood chairs _____ ?
2. made of / are / those / bowls / What _____ ?
3. Were / painted / those / wood figures / by hand _____ ?
4. was / painted / When / that / mural _____ ?
5. this / made in Thailand / gold jewelry / Was _____ ?
6. are / What / these / used for / cloth bags _____ ?

10 Look at the pictures. Write sentences to describe the objects. Use words from the box or your own ideas.

Material	clay	cloth	glass	gold	stone	wood
Adjective	beautiful impressive	boring interesting	cool practical	depressing terrific	fantastic weird	fascinating wonderful

1. _The hat is made of cloth. It's fantastic._
   _____

2. _____
   _____

3. _____
   _____

4. _____
   _____

5. _____
   _____

6. _____
   _____

sombrero hat, Mexico

bag, Spain

elephant figure, India

rocking chair, Canada

balalaika guitar, Russia

vase, France

The Arts   **W67**

11 Read the article about how to develop artistic talent.

Nurturing Your Artistic Talent

1 So, you'd like to improve your artistic ability, but you think you don't have any natural talent? The truth is you don't have to be born with talent to be a good artist—and to enjoy making art. Artistic skill can be learned.

2 Many people who try painting get frustrated and give up because they feel they lack the "artistic gene." However, the real problem is that they have just never been trained to look at the world like an artist. When non-artists look at the subject of a drawing, they see it with the left side of their brains. They immediately begin figuring out the meaning of what they see. An artist pays attention to what is actually being seen—the lines. Are they straight or curved? Dark or light? Where do they intersect?

3 Want to learn to see like an artist? Try this exercise. Find a large photo of a face and try to draw it. It's OK if your drawing looks bad. Then turn the photo upside down and try again. This time focus only on the relationships of the intersecting lines and shapes. Almost always, the upside-down drawing, when turned right side up, will be much better than the right-side-up version! How did this happen? By turning the photo upside down, the left side of your brain stopped looking at the photo as a face. Instead, the right side of your brain took over and began seeing the photo in a new way.

4 People who claim they have no artistic talent may actually have talent. But they may not be able to use it because they worry, "What will people think? Will I look silly? Will my piece be awful?" Young children rarely have these fears. They just enjoy the experience of creating something. To be successful at art, you will need to adopt the carefree attitude that you once had as a child. Don't worry about the results. Just relax and enjoy the experience of creating art.

5 Anyone can develop the necessary skills and understanding to create art. Those with natural talent are able to learn more quickly and easily, but even they will need training, practice, and hard work. So, stop making excuses and get started! Take art lessons, read books on art, and attend art exhibits. Expose yourself to a variety of techniques, kinds of art, and other artists. And think of becoming an artist as a lifetime journey. Stop worrying about making mistakes and enjoy the adventure!

Answer the questions, according to the article. Circle the letter.

1. What is the main idea of paragraph 2?
   a. Lacking the "artistic gene" is a real problem.
   b. You should always draw faces upside down.
   c. It's important to learn to see like an artist.
   d. Try to use the left side of your brain when you draw.

2. What is the main idea of paragraph 4?
   a. Children are better artists than adults.
   b. Fear of making mistakes prevents many adults from creating art.
   c. Fear helps adults find their artistic talent.
   d. Beginners' artwork is usually silly.

3. What is the main idea of paragraph 5?
   a. Artists with natural talent don't have to work hard.
   b. It takes a very long time to become a good artist.
   c. Artistic ability can be improved by attending art shows.
   d. Anyone can make art with practice and hard work.

12 Read the quotations by famous artists. Find a paragraph in the article that presents an opinion similar to that expressed by each artist. Write the number of the paragraph on the line.

1. ___   " Every child is an artist. The problem is how to remain an artist once we grow up. "
—Pablo Picasso

2. ___   " I am doubtful of any talent, so whatever I choose to be, will be accomplished only by long study and work. "
—Jackson Pollock

3. ___   " Creation begins with vision. The artist has to look at everything as though seeing it for the first time. "
—Henri Matisse

13 Read the third paragraph of the article again. Try the drawing exercise on a separate sheet of paper. Then answer the questions.

1. Which drawing was easier? _____

2. Which drawing took more time? _____

3. Which drawing looks more like the photograph? _____

4. Did the exercise help you to see more like an artist? Explain. _____

_____

14 Complete the biography of Pablo Picasso using the passive voice.

Pablo Ruiz Picasso began studying art with his father. Then from 1895 until 1904, he painted in Barcelona. During this time, he made his first trip to Paris, where he _____ by the
                                                                                        1. inspire
artwork of Henri de Toulouse-Lautrec. In Paris, Picasso _____ by all the poverty
                                                                2. influence
he saw. He was sad and angry that so many people lived without enough food or clothing. He painted many pictures of poor people to bring attention to their situation.

In 1906, Picasso met the artist Henri Matisse, who was to become his longtime friend. Picasso
_____ in Matisse's style, but he did not imitate it. The artists he really admired were
    3. interest
Georges Braque and Joan Miró. Picasso _____ by Braque's and Miró's work.
                                          4. fascinate
Together the three artists started the movement known as Cubism.

One of Picasso's most famous artistic pieces is
Guernica. Picasso _____ by the violence
                      5. move
of the Spanish Civil War. This prompted him to paint
the piece.

15 Read the biography again. Rewrite the five sentences in the passive voice,
changing them to the active voice.

1. _____
2. _____
3. _____
4. _____
5. _____

16 CHALLENGE. Write a short paragraph about your favorite kind of art and your favorite
artist. Use some of the phrases from the box.

interested in	fascinated by	inspired by	moved by	influenced by

A **If possible, rewrite the sentences, changing the active voice to the passive voice. If a sentence cannot be changed to the passive voice, circle the verb and write intransitive on the line.**

1. Leonardo da Vinci painted the *Mona Lisa* in the 16th century.

   _____

2. Pablo Picasso died in 1973 at 91 years old.

   _____

3. Paul Klee used simple lines and strong colors in his many paintings.

   _____

4. The artist's later work seems quite dark and depressing.

   _____

5. A new exhibit of impressionist paintings arrives at the Philadelphia Museum of Art this summer.

   _____

6. Marc Jacobs will show his spring collection at New York Fashion Week.

   _____

7. In Florence, we walked from The Uffizi Gallery to the Accademia Gallery to see Michelangelo's *David*.

   _____

B **Choose the best answer to complete each sentence. Circle the letter.**

1. This vase _____ made in 1569.
   a. is   **b.** has been   **c.** was   **d.** was being

2. Today, coffee _____ grown in more than fifty countries worldwide.
   a. has been   **b.** will be   **c.** was   **d.** is

3. Right now, business cards _____ exchanged at the meeting.
   a. were   **b.** were being   **c.** are being   **d.** have been

4. The art exhibition _____ attended by over 1,000 people so far.
   a. was   **b.** has been   **c.** is going to be   **d.** is being

5. We probably _____ invited to the wedding. It's going to be very small.
   a. won't be   **b.** weren't being   **c.** haven't been   **d.** weren't

C **Use the words to write sentences in the passive voice.**

1. French / speak / in Quebec, Canada _____

2. The Taj Mahal / build / around 1631 _____

3. A new art museum / open / next year _____

4. Many products / make / in China _____

5. "Imagine" / write / by John Lennon _____

6. Your DVD player / repair / now _____

7. The *Mona Lisa* / see / by millions of people since it was painted _____

   _____

D Read the description of a museum. Find and correct four more mistakes in the use of the passive voice.

The Frick Collection

The mansion of Henry Clay Frick ~~builded~~ *was built* in 1914 at the corner of Fifth Avenue and East 70th Street in New York City. It was later open to the public. Several improvements have made over the years. Works of Manet, El Greco, Bernini, Degas, Vermeer, and many other artists found throughout the mansion. Some of the museum's large collection of art displayed at temporary exhibitions around the world.

E Rewrite the sentences in the passive voice. Use a <u>by</u> phrase only if it is important or necessary to know who or what is performing the action.

1. People in Guatemala carved this wood figure.

   _____

2. Artists hand-paint these plates in France.

   _____

3. Valentino is showing a lot of bright colors this season.

   _____

4. Stores everywhere are going to sell her jewelry.

   _____

5. Swiss companies still make the world's best watches.

   _____

6. Shakespeare wrote *King Lear*.

   _____

F Rewrite the sentences in the passive voice in Exercise E as <u>yes / no</u> questions.

1. _Was this wood figure carved in Guatemala?_____
2. _____
3. _____
4. _____
5. _____
6. _____

A Read the paragraph. Underline the topic sentence. Circle the supporting details. Cross out the two sentences that don't belong.

I have been to museums in countries all over the world, but my favorite painting is in a museum close to my home. I am a real fan of *The Master's Bedroom* by Andrew Wyeth because I find it very peaceful. Andrew Wyeth died in 2009 at the age of 91. The painting shows a dog curled up on a bed, taking an afternoon nap. Sunlight is coming in through the window and warming the dog. The painting makes me feel relaxed because the dog and the bed look so comfortable. The bedroom is very simple, and the colors in the painting are soft and neutral, making the scene seem really calm. Wyeth's most famous painting is *Christina's World*, which is at the Museum of Modern Art in New York City.

B Think about your favorite painting. Answer the questions.

1. What is the title of the painting? _____

2. Who is the artist? _____

3. Why do you like it? _____

_____

C Prepare to describe your favorite painting in a paragraph. Create a topic sentence and supporting details.

a. What is the most important thing you want to say about the painting?

_____

b. Write five sentences to support your topic sentence.

1. _____

2. _____

3. _____

4. _____

5. _____

D On a separate sheet of paper, write a paragraph describing your favorite painting. Feel free to change the order of your sentences or add more details if you think it would improve your writing.

1 **Read the Photo Story on page 99 of the Student's Book again. Then answer the questions.**

1. What computer problem does Amy have? _____

_____

2. What solution does Dee suggest? _____

_____

2 **Read the instant message conversation. Then answer the questions.**

ron22: Hey, Deb. Are you there?

dpike: Hi, Ron. Just catching up on e-mail.

ron22: Am I interrupting you?

dpike: Not at all. What's up?

ron22: I just emailed you some pictures.

dpike: Great! What of?

ron22: Photos of my trip!!!

dpike: Cool! Can't wait to see them.

ron22: It'll just be a second . . .

B I U A A ᴀ A A   ♫ ♥   SEND

a few minutes later

dpike: Hi Ron. Still there? I didn't get the pix.

ron22: Sorry! I attached the photos, but I can't send the message. It says the files are too large!

dpike: Maybe you should try sending them one at a time.

ron22: You think that would work?

dpike: It usually does the trick.

ron22: OK, I'll try it.

B I U A A ᴀ A A   ♫ ♥   SEND

1. What computer problem does Ron have? _____

_____

2. What solution does Deb suggest? _____

_____

3 Which of the following computer problems have you experienced?

- ☐ computer won't start
- ☐ lost a file
- ☐ printer won't print
- ☐ computer is slowing down
- ☐ got a computer virus
- ☐ forgot a password
- ☐ keyboard freezes
- ☐ mouse doesn't work
- ☐ can't attach a file

4 CHALLENGE. Have you ever asked someone for help with a computer problem? If so, who did you ask? What solution did the person suggest?

5 Choose the correct response. Circle the letter.

1. "What are you doing here at this hour?"
   a. Nothing happens.　　b. Running antivirus software.　　c. I've never had a problem before.

2. "Am I interrupting you?"
   a. Of course.　　b. Right.　　c. Not at all.

3. "When I try to click on an icon, my computer freezes and won't do anything."
   a. It couldn't hurt.　　b. Sometimes that does the trick.　　c. Maybe you should try restarting.

4. "You think that would fix the problem?"
   a. It couldn't hurt.　　b. I'll just be a second.　　c. Sorry to hear that.

LESSON 1

6 Use the icon prompts to complete the conversation. Write the word on the line.

A: Could you take a look at this?

B: Sure. What's the problem?

A: Well, I clicked on the toolbar to _____ 1. my document, and now everything is gone!

B: Don't worry. You probably accidentally clicked on the _____ 2. icon. Just move your cursor over there and click on this icon to _____ 3. it.

A: Oh . . . There it is! Thank you!

7 Complete each sentence with a word from the box.

| click on | cut | paste | print | save | scroll down | select | toolbar |

1. Oh, no! I just lost all the work I've done on this document because I forgot to _____ the file.

2. You can't _____ if the printer is not turned on.

3. To _____ a word, move the cursor over the word and highlight it.

4. You don't have to type the entire paragraph again. Just copy and _____ it where you need it.

5. I tried to _____ the icon but nothing happened. What did I do wrong?

6. The _____ has a list of icons that provide a quick way to use computer commands.

7. To see more information on the product, _____ to the bottom of the page.

8. Your article is great but a little too long. Could you _____ a few paragraphs?

8 Match each action with the correct purpose. Write the letter on the line.

1. _____ He enrolled in an electronics course because he . . .   a. needed to buy a printer.

2. _____ She went to the electronics store because she . . .   b. needed to be more organized.

3. _____ I bought speakers because I . . .   c. wanted to learn how to repair computers.

4. _____ He turned on the television because he . . .   d. wanted to listen to music on the computer.

5. _____ She bought a smart phone because she . . .   e. wanted to watch the news.

9 Rewrite the sentences in Exercise 8, using infinitives of purpose.

1. _____
2. _____
3. _____
4. _____
5. _____

LESSON 2

10 Put the conversation in order. Write the number on the line.

_1_ I was wondering if you could help me with something.

_____ Why don't you get an OptiMouse? I have one, and I really like it.

_____ Well, I'm thinking about buying a new mouse, but I'm not sure which one to get.

_____ Then how about the UltraClick? It's nearly as easy to use as the OptiMouse, but it doesn't cost quite as much.

_____ Of course. What's up?

_____ I like the OptiMouse, but it's a little expensive.

_7_ Sounds good. I'll have to check it out.

11 Look at the chart comparing two laptop computers. Complete the sentences, using (not) as . . . as and the adjectives. Use the adverbs <u>almost</u>, <u>quite</u>, <u>just</u>, and <u>nearly</u>.

	Ace EC650u laptop	Simsun B400 laptop
Price	$619	$599
Weight	5 pounds / 2.3 kilograms	3 pounds / 1.4 kilograms
Screen size	16 inches / 40.6 centimeters	15.5 inches / 39.4 centimeters
Screen quality	◑	◑
Touchpad ease of use	●	◑
Speed	●	◑
Speaker quality	●	●
Noise	◑	◑

KEY

Better
●
↕
◑
○
Worse

1. The quality of the Ace screen is _____*just as good as*_____ the quality of the Simsun screen.
   <u>good</u>
2. The Simsun laptop is _____ the Ace laptop.
   <u>expensive</u>
3. The Simsun touchpad isn't _____ the Ace touchpad.
   <u>easy to use</u>
4. The Simsun laptop is _____ the Ace laptop.
   <u>fast</u>
5. The Ace speakers are _____ the Simsun speakers.
   <u>good</u>
6. The Ace laptop isn't _____ the Simsun laptop.
   <u>light</u>
7. The Simsun screen isn't _____ the Ace screen.
   <u>large</u>

12 **CHALLENGE.** Which laptop in Exercise 11 would you buy? Explain your reasons, using (not) as . . . as and some of the adverbs from Exercise 11.

13 **Read about how the people use computers. Complete the statements with words from the box.**

send instant messages	surf the Internet	join an online group
upload photos	download music files	

1.

" I'm a designer, and I really need to learn about what people wear and why they wear it. So I decided to _____ called Fashion Friends. On the website, I discuss clothing trends and style with other members. **"**

2.

" I have a lot of friends, and I like to be in touch with them all the time. Talking on the phone isn't always practical, and e-mail is too slow. So, my friends and I _____ to each other all the time. **"**

3.

" I'm a huge music fan, but I never buy CDs at a music store. I _____ from the Internet, instead. I've got almost 10,000 songs on my MP3 player now! **"**

4.

" I'm spending two months traveling through Europe. I want my friends and family to see all the fascinating places I'm visiting, so I _____ from my laptop to a website where everyone can view them. **"**

5.

" I spend about eight hours a day online. I usually just _____, clicking from one website to another without any real plan. I love to discover new and different websites about things that interest me. **"**

14 **CHALLENGE. On a separate sheet of paper, write a paragraph about how you use computers. Be sure to answer the following questions.**

- How many hours a week do you spend on a computer?
- Do you spend more or less time on a computer than your friends or family members?
- Do you use a computer more for work or for fun?
- What do you use a computer to do?

15 Read the article from a career advice website.

Social Networking: Could It Hurt Your Job Search?

To be the best candidate for a job, you'll need more than an impressive résumé and a nice suit. You also need to make sure there isn't any information about you online that could cause an employer not to hire you. A recent study found that 77 percent of recruiters search the Internet for information about applicants they are considering for a job. Thirty-five percent of these same recruiters say they have rejected an applicant based on information they have found online.

"A profile on a social networking site can show you a lot more of a person's character than a résumé," says Jen Romney, a corporate recruiter who recently began looking up the names of applicants on the Web. "It's surprising what you can find. I once had to make a difficult decision between two excellent applicants. When I found one of the applicants' profile on a social networking site, the decision became much easier. The man's profile was full of negative comments about his job and boss. In one post he wrote, 'I'm calling in sick today—because I'm sick of work!' I don't need to tell you that he didn't get the job."

Romney warns that as people share more of their lives online, it becomes harder to keep one's private life completely private. "Everything is public," says Romney. "It's called the World Wide Web for a reason. Anyone in the world can see it."

While not all employers research potential employees online, it's worth being a little careful to make sure that social networking doesn't ruin your career opportunities. You can protect yourself by following four simple rules:

1. **Think before you click.** Before you post photos of you and your friends partying or comments about how you hate your job, ask yourself: Would I be comfortable talking about this in a job interview?

2. **Take control.** Most social networking sites have privacy controls. Take the time to figure them out and use them wisely. Set your controls so that only people you've chosen as "friends" can view your profile and post messages on your page.

3. **Review.** Check your profile regularly to see what has been posted. Type your name and e-mail address into a search engine to see what is on the Internet about you.

4. **Delete.** Remove any potentially embarrassing or offensive posts, information, or photos. Ask friends to delete anything inappropriate about you on their own profiles.

Use the context of the article to match the terms with their meanings.

1. _____ recruiter
2. _____ search engine
3. _____ profile
4. _____ post
5. _____ private

a. only for a particular group to see, not for everyone
b. information, photos, comments, etc. put on a website
c. a person who finds candidates to fill jobs
d. page on a social networking site with a member's personal information
e. a program that helps you find things on the Internet

16 Answer the questions, according to the information in the article in Exercise 15.

1. How does the Internet make it easier for employers to get information about job applicants?

_____

_____

2. What type of information in an online profile can hurt a job applicant's chances of getting a job?

_____

_____

3. What is one way you can control who is able to view your online profiles?

_____

_____

4. How can you learn what information is available about you online?

_____

_____

17 **CHALLENGE.** Do you think the article on page 79 gives good advice? What have you done, or what do you plan to do, to protect your image online? Explain your answer.

GRAMMAR BOOSTER

A Read the conversation. Find all the infinitives that express a purpose. Underline the sentences.

A: It's 6:00. Are you going home?

B: No, I'm staying late to finish this report. How about you?

A: I'm leaving now. I'm going to stop at Big Box to buy a new printer. Then I'm going to ComputerWorld to get something else on sale.

B: Really? What?

A: I'm thinking about getting a new laptop.

B: What's wrong with your home computer?

A: Nothing. But the kids use it to surf the Internet all the time.

B: What do they do online?

A: Oh, everything. They use the computer to check e-mail, download music, chat with their friends, and play games.

B Rewrite the sentences you underlined in Exercise A. Use <u>in order to</u>.

1. _____
2. _____
3. _____
4. _____
5. _____

C Rewrite Speaker A's last sentence in Exercise A, using <u>for</u>. (Remember to change the verbs into gerunds.)

_____

_____

D Complete the sentences with <u>for</u> or <u>to</u>.

1. I like to shop online _____ delicious foods from Italy.

2. My son uses the computer _____ download music.

3. Judith e-mailed me _____ directions to the party.

4. Daniel uses the Internet _____ get the latest news.

5. Sheila e-mailed her mother _____ say she bought a new computer.

E Complete the sentences. Use an infinitive of purpose or <u>for</u>.

1. I use the Internet _____.

2. I'd buy a new printer _____.

3. I'd get a new smart phone _____.

F Complete each sentence with the correct form of the adjective or adverb.

1. I shop online for computer products. It's much _____ than going to a computer store.
   easy

2. My brother plays music _____ than anyone I know.
   loudly

3. Of all the printers in the store, the R100 is definitely the _____.
   quiet

4. This is the _____ movie I've ever seen.
   romantic

5. Jessica's oil paintings are beautiful. Her pencil drawings are just as _____.
   impressive

6. Believe it or not, this new laptop works as _____ as the old one.
   badly

7. The Bax monitor is not large enough. I need something even _____.
   big

8. The traffic on my way to work was very slow. Luckily, the traffic on my way home was not nearly as

   _____.
   bad

9. We've never had a _____ vacation than this one. It was so much fun!
   exciting

10. Of the three printers we looked at, the XP prints the _____.
    poorly

G Look at the video game reviews. Write sentences comparing the A–1 and Game Plan games. Use the comparative form of the adjective or adverb.

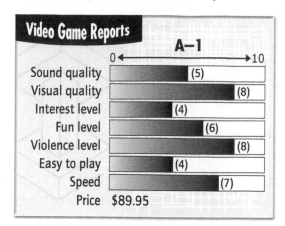

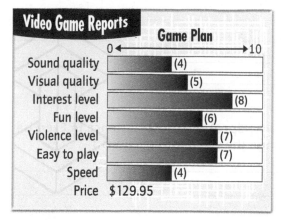

1. A–1 sounds _better than_____ Game Plan.
   _{good}

2. A–1 looks _____ Game Plan.
   _{good}

3. Game Plan is _____ A–1.
   _{interesting}

4. Game Plan is _____ A–1.
   _{violent}

5. Game Plan is _____ A–1.
   _{easy to play}

6. Game Plan runs _____ A–1.
   _{slow}

7. A–1 is _____ Game Plan.
   _{expensive}

H Now look at the review of a third video game. Write sentences comparing all three video games, using the superlative form of the adjective or adverb.

1. _Top Game sounds the best._____
   _{good}

2. _____
   _{expensive}

3. _____
   _{fast}

4. _____
   _{easy to play}

5. _____
   _{interesting}

6. _____
   _{violent}

Video Game Reports — **Top Game**

	0 ← → 10
Sound quality	(8)
Visual quality	(8)
Interest level	(2)
Fun level	(2)
Violence level	(5)
Easy to play	(3)
Speed	(8)
Price	$199.95

A Read the ideas for a piece of writing about the pros and cons of social networking. Then write each idea in the appropriate place on the chart.

Ideas

- It's a great way to keep in touch with friends and family all over the world.
- You can find old friends and people you've lost contact with.
- It may be too entertaining—it's easy to waste a lot of time on social networking sites.
- Your friends may post photos or comments you'd rather not have others see.
- People you don't want to keep in touch with (like an old boyfriend or girlfriend) may ask to be your friend.
- Social networking is entertaining—and, on some sites, you can also play games and take fun quizzes.

Topic	Ideas	
1. communicating with family and friends	Pros	
	Cons	
2. getting back in touch with old friends	Pros	
	Cons	
3. is entertaining	Pros	
	Cons	

B On a separate sheet of paper, write two paragraphs about "The Pros and Cons of Social Networking." Use Approach 2 from page 147 in the Student's Book. Use the ideas from the "Pros" row of the chart in paragraph 1. Use the ideas from the "Cons" row of the chart in paragraph 2. Create your own topic sentence for each paragraph.

C On a separate sheet of paper, use Approach 3 from page 147 in the Student's Book. Use the ideas from row 1 of the chart in paragraph 1, the ideas from row 2 in paragraph 2, and the ideas from row 3 in paragraph 3. Create your own topic sentence for each paragraph. Use <u>In addition</u> and <u>Furthermore</u> to add your own ideas.

1   Read the messages to an advice columnist. What advice do you think
    the columnist will give? Check the box.

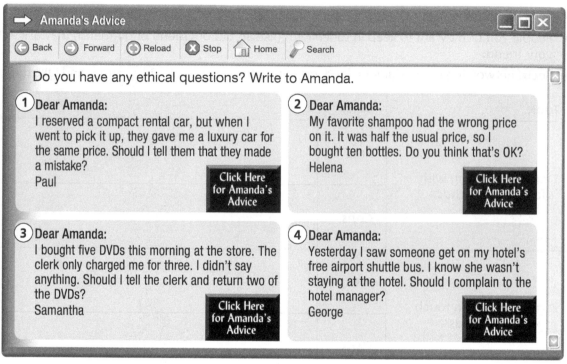

1. ☐ Paul should tell the rental company they made a mistake and offer to pay for the luxury car.

    ☐ Paul should stop worrying and enjoy his luxury car.

2. ☐ Helena should feel great about saving money.

    ☐ Helena should go back and tell the store manager the price was wrong and pay the correct price.

3. ☐ Samantha should tell the clerk that she wasn't charged for two of the DVDs.

    ☐ Samantha should just relax and enjoy the DVDs without telling the clerk.

4. ☐ George should tell the hotel manager about the person using the shuttle bus.

    ☐ George should mind his own business and not complain about someone else.

2   **CHALLENGE. Have you ever experienced a moral dilemma similar to the ones
    described in Exercise 1? Write a letter to Amanda about your situation.**

3   **Read the conversations. Summarize the advice with real conditional sentences.**

1. **A:** I don't have antivirus software.
   B: You shouldn't surf the Internet.

   If you don't have antivirus software, you shouldn't surf the Internet.

2. **A:** I want to e-mail old photos to friends.
   B: You have to scan them first.

   _____

3. **A:** I want to make friends on the Internet.
   B: You can join an online group.

   _____

4. **A:** My computer crashes all the time.
   B: You'd better find out what's wrong.

   _____

4   **Rewrite the real conditional sentences in the unreal conditional. Use the true statements in parentheses to help you.**

1. If we go to Russia, I'll learn Russian. (We're not going to Russia.)

   _____

2. If she has time, she'll study more. (She doesn't have time.)

   _____

3. If I need to lose weight, I'll avoid fatty foods. (I don't need to lose weight.)

   _____

4. If he's late, he won't get a seat. (He's never late.)

   _____

5   **Match the two parts of each conditional sentence. Write the letter on the line.**

1. _____ If you speak Spanish, you . . .
2. _____ If you spoke Spanish, you . . .
3. _____ Your hair will look great if you . . .
4. _____ He would look great if he . . .
5. _____ If you took a taxi, you . . .
6. _____ If you miss the bus, you . . .
7. _____ You'll get sunburned if you . . .
8. _____ We would get sunburned if we . . .

a. don't use sunscreen.
b. could work in South America.
c. won't get to work on time.
d. stayed at the beach too long.
e. use this shampoo every day.
f. can travel all over Central America.
g. got a haircut.
h. would get to work faster.

6 Complete each present unreal conditional sentence. Use your own ideas.

   1. If I lived to be 100, _____.

   2. My family would be angry if _____.

   3. If I went to my favorite store, _____.

7 Look at the pictures. Use the words and phrases in the box to complete the conversations.

too much change	undercharged	didn't charge

   1. A: Look at this bill.

   B: What's wrong with it?

   A: They _____ us. Look.
   They _____ us for the drinks
   or for the desserts.

   B: I guess we'd better tell them.

   2. A: What's wrong?

   B: I think the clerk gave me _____.
   I should have only two euros back in change,
   but she gave me twelve!

   A: I'll try to get her attention . . . Excuse me?

LESSON 2

8 Circle the correct words to complete the conversations.

   1. A: Where should we watch the game after work?

   B: Let's go to your house. (Your / Yours) TV is much bigger than (my / mine).

   2. A: Is this (our / ours) room?

   B: No, we have a suite, and this is a single. So, this is definitely not (our / ours).

   3. A: Is this car key (your / yours)?

   B: No, it's not (my / mine). I don't even have a car!

   4. A: (Who / Whose) books are these? (Him / His) or (her / hers)?

   B: I don't know. Ask them if they're (their / theirs).

   5. A: (Who / Whose) has traveled more? Your parents or (mine / my)?

   B: (Your / Yours) parents, I think. (My / Mine) parents don't travel much at all.

9 Rewrite each sentence, using a possessive pronoun.

1. The shaving cream is George's. ___The shaving cream is his.___

2. The hair spray is Judy's. _____

3. The toothbrushes are Amy and Mark's. _____

4. The razors are George's. _____

5. The shampoo is everyone's. _____

10 Look at the pictures. Complete the conversations with possessive adjectives or possessive pronouns.

1. **A:** Excuse me. I think you forgot something.

   B: I did?

   A: Isn't that cell phone _____?

   B: No, it isn't. It must be _____.

2. **A:** Is this _____?

   B: No, it's not _____.

   It's _____ tip.

3. **A:** Is that book _____?

   B: No, it's _____ book.

4. **A:** Are these earrings _____?

   B: No, they're not _____.

   They're _____.

11 Read about the people's personal values. How would you describe each person? Use words from the box or your own words. Explain your opinions.

modesty	sexist	old-fashioned	double-standard

James

> I hate having a female boss. I just don't think women make good managers.

_____

_____

_____

Dina

> I'm not comfortable wearing clothes that show too much of my body.

_____

_____

_____

Tessa

> I think it's fine for young men and women to get their bodies pierced if they want to. But if you're over forty, you really shouldn't. It just looks silly!

_____

_____

_____

Hazel

> People used to dress formally when they went to the opera. Now some people wear jeans. It's just not appropriate!

_____

_____

_____

12 **CHALLENGE.** Choose one person from Exercise 11. Do you have the same values? Explain why or why not.

13 Read the news stories on page 118 of the Student's Book again. Then answer the questions.

1. How did Kim Bogue lose her wallet? _____
   _____

2. How did the homeless man return the wallet to her? _____
   _____

3. What happened to Cameron Hollopeter? _____
   _____

4. What did Wesley Autrey do? _____
   _____

5. How did the airport screener figure out who the money belonged to? _____
   _____

14 Read the news story about an act of honesty.

Pro Golfer J. P. Hayes's Act of Honesty

J. P. Hayes is a professional golfer. But Hayes has perhaps gotten more attention for an act of honesty than for his golf game. While playing in the first round of a PGA tournament in Texas, Hayes' caddie handed him a ball from his golf bag. Hayes took two shots and then noticed the ball he was playing with was a different model than the ball he started the round with. This is against the rules in professional golf. So, Hayes asked an official to come over and told him about his mistake. The official said the penalty for the mistake was two shots. Even with the penalty, Hayes finished with a good score. He also did well in the second round and had a good chance of advancing to the final. Hayes had struggled with his game that year, so this tournament was important to his career.

After the second round of the tournament, Hayes was relaxing in his hotel room when he realized there might be another problem with the ball he played in the first round. He realized it was a new type of ball that probably wasn't approved for competition by the United States Golf Association. Hayes had tested the new balls for a golf equipment company four weeks earlier. Apparently, one was left in his bag by accident.

Hayes knew that if he admitted his mistake, he would probably not be allowed to play full-time on the next year's PGA tour. He also knew that no one else was aware of his mistake. Hayes had a choice: He could say nothing and keep playing, or he could admit that he had broken the rules and hurt his career.

Hayes decided to do the right thing. He called an official that night and, as expected, was disqualified from playing on the next PGA tour. Speaking about his mistake, Hayes said "It's extremely disappointing. I keep thinking I'm going to wake up and this is

going to be a bad nightmare." However, Hayes never regretted his decision. "I would say everybody out here would have done the same thing," he asserted. But the real question is: Would they? In a similar situation, would other professional athletes have acted as honestly as J. P. Hayes?

Answer the questions, according to the article.

1. What was the first mistake Hayes made? _____

2. What was the second mistake Hayes made? _____
_____

3. Did anyone see Hayes make the mistakes? _____
_____

4. What happened when Hayes told officials about the first mistake? _____
_____

5. What happened when Hayes told officials about the second mistake? _____
_____

15 **CHALLENGE. Imagine that you were in J. P. Hayes's situation. Answer the questions.**

1. What could you do?	
2. What should you do?	
3. What would you do?	
4. What would most people do?	

GRAMMAR BOOSTER

A **Read the statements and then complete the factual conditional sentences.**

1. I usually go jogging every day, unless it rains.

   If it doesn't rain, _I go jogging_____.

2. I like driving short distances, but for longer distances, I always fly.

   _____ if I have to travel longer distances.

3. I never drink coffee after dinner. I can't fall asleep when I do.

   _____, I can't fall asleep at night.

4. It rarely snows here. The schools close whenever more than an inch falls.

   _____ if it snows more than an inch.

5. I never watch horror movies before bed. I just can't get to sleep!

   _____, I can't get to sleep.

B Rewrite the factual conditional sentences in Exercise A, reversing the clauses and using commas where necessary.

1. _____ I go jogging if it doesn't rain. _____

2. _____

3. _____

4. _____

5. _____

C Choose the correct form to complete each present or future factual conditional sentence.

1. If they (like / will like) the musical, they (see / will see) it again tomorrow.

2. Whenever Fernando (watched / watches) comedies, he (laughed / laughs).

3. If you (buy / will buy) some ice cream, I (help / will help) you eat it.

4. When I (won't / don't) fall asleep, I usually (get / got) a lot of work done in the evening.

5. (Will you / Do you) travel to England if your boss (needs / will need) you there next month?

6. Always (wear / wore) your seat belt if you (want / will want) to be safe.

7. I (didn't get / won't get) a tattoo if my parents (tell / told) me not to.

8. If I (ask / will ask) my brother for help, he (say / will say) no.

9. Whenever I (travel / will travel) far, I always (fly / flew) first class.

D Complete the sentences, using the appropriate possessive nouns.

1. The _____ tip is still on the table.
        waiter

2. _____ wallet was stolen when he was on vacation.
        Lucas

3. The _____ new computer cost them an arm and a leg.
        Browns

4. If the _____ team wins tonight, they'll be in the championships.
        women

5. They undercharged me for _____ present.
                Tom and Audrey

6. Whose money is this? Is it _____ ?
                Lucy

7. Whenever I travel, I borrow my _____ suitcase.
                parents

8. My aunt and uncle don't care for my _____ tattoo.
                cousin

E Answer the questions, using pronouns in place of the underlined nouns and noun phrases. The answers to the questions are in Unit 10. Check the Student's Book page in parentheses.

1. Did <u>Matt</u> break <u>the plate</u>? (page 111)

   Yes, he broke it.

2. Is <u>Matt</u> going to tell <u>the owner</u>? (page 111)

   _____

3. Did <u>the waiter</u> charge <u>the husband and wife</u> for <u>their desserts</u>? (page 113)

   _____

4. Did <u>a customer</u> return <u>the jacket</u> to <u>the child and her father</u>? (page 114)

   _____

5. Did <u>the homeless man</u> keep <u>the wallet he found</u>? (page 118)

   _____

6. Did <u>the "subway hero"</u> know <u>the passenger he saved</u>? (page 118)

   _____

7. Did <u>the airport screener</u> give <u>the bag of money</u> back to <u>its owner</u>? (page 118)

   _____

WRITING BOOSTER

A Choose a situation from page 119 of the Student's Book. Write the situation on the line.

_____

B On a separate sheet of paper, write a paragraph about what you could do in that situation, if you didn't act with kindness or honesty. For example, discuss the advantages of keeping money you found or not paying for something.

C Now write a second paragraph about what you should do in that situation. Begin your paragraph with <u>On the other hand</u>.

D Read your paragraphs. Circle the paragraph that describes what you think most people would do. Put a star next to the paragraph that describes what you would do.

Student Book

Photo credits: Original photography by Sharon Hoogstraten, David Mager and Libby Ballengee/TSI Graphics. Page 62 (tl bg) Ilya Zaytsev/Fotolia, (tl) D. Hurst/Alamy, (tr bg) Ilya Zaytsev/Fotolia, (tl) D. Hurst/Alamy, (butter) Coleman Yuen/Pearson Education Asia Ltd, (Fork) Vo/Fotolia, (m bg) Ilya Zaytsev/Fotolia, (Fruit) Koszivu/Fotolia, (Bread,grains,pasta) Nikcy Petkov/Shutterstock, (Vegetables) Ana Blazic Pavlovic/Shutterstock, (Meat,fish,beans) D. Hurst/Alamy, (green napkin) Karandaev/Fotolia, (placemat) Aleksandr Ugorenkov / Folia; p. 63 (Mushroom diet) Viktor/Fotolia, (Vegan diet) Studio Gi/Fotolia, (Atkins diet) Vladimir Melnik/Fotolia, (Juice Fast) Larisa Lofitskaya/Shutterstock; p. 64 (Sushi) Motorlka/Fotolia, (Mangoes) Volff/Fotolia, (Pasta) Vagabondo/Fotolia, (Ice cream) Unpict/Fotolia, (Asparagus) Africa Studio/Fotolia; p. 67 (Octopus) Denio109/Fotolia, (Shellfish) Maceo/Fotolia, (Tofu) Lilyana Vynogradova/Fotolia, (Steak) Joe Gough/Fotolia, (Broccoli) Ping Han/Fotolia, (Beets) Mitev/Fotolia, (Chocolate) Taigl/Fotolia; p. 68 (tr) Fotandy/Shutterstock, (br) Saje/Fotolia; p. 69 Apollofoto/Shutterstock; p. 70 (a) Shakzu/Fotolia, (Grasshopper) Valeriy Kirsanov/Fotolia, (b) Paul Brighton/Fotolia, (c) Nattawut Thammasak/Fotolia, (d) Africa Studio/Fotolia, (e) Vankad/ Fotolia, (f) Uckyo/Fotolia, (Cabbage) Nomad Soul/Fotolia; p. 71 (1,2,3,4) Mariusz Blach/Fotolia, (br) Mourad/Tarek/ Bon Appetit/Alamy; p. 73 (Pad Thai) Narith_2527/iStock/Thinkstock/ Getty Images, (Bi Bim Bop) Ain Bagwell/Photodisc/Getty Images, (Chicken Mole) Uckyo/Fotolia, (Potato Soup) Juanmonino/E+/Getty Images, (Tabouleh Salad) M.studio/Fotolia, (Pot Stickers) Chiyacat/Fotolia, (br) Yuris/Shutterstock; p. 74 Lightboxx/Shutterstock; p. 78 Imagesource/Glow Images; p. 79 LightWaveMedia/Shutterstock; p. 80 Pavel L Photo and Video/ Shutterstock; p. 81 (tr) Zsschreiner/Shutterstock, (bl) Taka/Fotolia, (br) Eurobanks/Fotolia; p. 82 Monkey Business Images/Shutterstock; p. 83 (t) Rob/Fotolia, (b) Tanya Constantine/Blend/ Corbis; p. 85 (1) WaveBreakMedia/Shutterstock, (2) Jeremy Woodhouse/Blend Images/Getty Images, (3) Corey Rich/Aurora/Getty Images; p. 86 (Jewelry) Harshmunjal/Fotolia, (Fashion) Terex/Fotolia, (Pottery) Africa Studio/Fotolia, (Painting) Boyan Dimitrov/Shutterstock, (Photography) Philippova Anastasia/Shutterstock; p. 87 (ml) Boyan Dimitrov/Fotolia, (m) Gurgen Bakhshetsyan/Shutterstock, (mr) Rozaliya/Fotolia, (mr) Nils Volkmer/Shutterstock; p. 89 (Monalisa) Dennis Hallinan/Alamy, (Gold Museum) *Cacique Guatavita, known as El Dorado's raft in gold and emeralds, Colombia, Chibcha civilization (or Muisca)*/De Agostini Picture Library/G. Dagli Orti/Bridgeman Images, (National Palace Museum) *Chinese cabbage, Korean, 19th century (jade)* / National Palace Museum, Taipei, Taiwan/ Bridgeman Images, (Museum of Modern Art) GL Archive/Alamy; p. 90 (Wood) Pavel K/Shutterstock, (Glass) Sagir/Shutterstock, (Silver) Nolte Lourens/Fotolia, (Gold ring)Lynnette/Fotolia; (Cloth) NH7/Fotolia, (Ceramic) Deborah McCague/Shutterstock, (Stone) Winnond/Shutterstock; p. 91 (Vase) Nikonbhoy/Fotolia, (Plate) Piero Gentili/Fotolia, (Dolls) Ketsur/Fotolia, (Figure) Kanvag/Fotolia, (Cups) Mrpuili/Shutterstock; p. 92 Audrey Benson; p. 93 Africa Studio/Fotolia; p. 94 (Stella) AFP/Newscom, (Vincent) De Agostini Picture Library/Getty Images, (Charles) Picture-alliance/Newscom, (Valentino) Splash News/Newscom, (Frida) Bettmann/Corbis, (Henri) Charles Platiau/Reuters/ Newscom, (Ang Lee) Fox 2000 Pictures/Album/Newscom; p. 95 (l) Nicholas Piccillo/Fotolia, (m) Michael Jung/Shutterstock, (r) Arek Malang/Shutterstock; p. 96 (a) Pytralona/Shutterstock, (b) Swisshippo/Fotolia, (c) Nerthuz/Fotolia, (d) www.TouchofArt.eu/Fotolia, (e) Yezep/Fotolia; p. 97 (Accademia Gallery) Akg-Images/Cameraphoto/Newscom, (David) Ndphoto/ Shutterstock, (Musee d'Orsay) Brian Jannsen/Alamy, (Apples and Oranges) *Apples and Oranges, 1895-1900 (oil on canvas), Cezanne, Paul (1839-1906)*/Musee d'Orsay, Paris, France/ Giraudon/Bridgeman Images, (Peru) Eduardo Rivero/Shutterstock, (India)Сергей Чирков/Fotolia, (China) Stockphoto Mania/Shutterstock, (Sweden) Tobyphotos/Shutterstock; p. 98 (Frank) Yulia Mayorova/Shutterstock, (Kathy) Phototalk/E+/Getty Images, (Nardo) Warren Goldswain/Fotolia; p. 100 (tr) Blue Images/Ivy/Corbis, (Monitor,screen) Antiksu/Fotolia, (Mouse) Violetkaipa/Shutterstock, (Touchpad) Tagore75/Fotolia; p. 102 Nikkytok/Fotolia; p. 103 (Joystick) Geargodz/Fotolia, StockLite/Shutterstock; p. 104 (4) Hero Images/Getty Images; p. 106 Chanpipat/Shutterstock; p. 107 (l) Glow Images/Getty Images, (r) Kitty/Shutterstock; p. 109 (ml) Olix Wirtinger/Fancy/Corbis; p. 115 (Book) Irina Burakova/Fotolia, (Smartphone) Bloomua/Fotolia, (Wallet) Grigoriy Lukyanov/Fotolia, (Coat) Ludmilafoto/Fotolia, (Headphones) Alexander Demyanenko/Fotolia, (Gloves) Spe/Fotolia, (Bag) Nikolai Sorokin/Fotolia; p. 116 (l) Jaroslav Kviz/Profimedia.CZ a.s./Alamy; (m) Tristan Savatier/Moment/Getty Images, (r) AnnaDe/Shutterstock; p. 117 Underwood Photo Archives/Superstock; p. 118 Bikeworldtravel/Fotolia.

Illustration credits: Steve Attoe, p. 64; John Ceballos, p. 121; Andy Myer, p. 66; Dusan Petricic, pp. 70, 78, 79, 113; Neil Stewart, p. 119 (center, bottom); Anne Veltfort, pp. 66 (top-right), 119 (top).

Text credits: Page 74: *Psychology of Color* from infoplease.com. Reprinted with permission.

Workbook

Photo credits: Original photography by David Mager. Page W49 Andres Rodriguez/Fotolia; p. W50 kasto/Fotolia; p. W64 (left) Mikhail Zahranichny/Fotolia, (right) rubtsov89/ Fotolia; p. W66 Serge Vero/Shutterstock; p. W67 (top left) Vice and Virtue/Fotolia, (top right) Comugnero Silvana/Fotolia, (middle left) Dmitri Mikitenko/Fotolia, (middle right) glarson/ Fotolia, (bottom left) blacklionder/Fotolia, (bottom right) Simon Curtis/Alamy; p. W68 Africa Studio/Shutterstock; p. W69 (top) Everett Collection Inc/Alamy, (middle) Tony Vaccaro/Archive Photos/Getty Images, (bottom) INTERFOTO/Alamy; p. W70 DPA/ABACA/Newscom; p. W74 (left) gstockstudio/Fotolia, (right) Elenathewise/Fotolia; p. W77 (left) EDHAR/Shutterstock, (right) unclepodger/Fotolia; p. W78 (1) Maskot/Getty Images, (2) apops/Fotolia, (3) leungchopan/Shutterstock, (4) WavebreakmediaMicro/Fotolia, (5) micromonkey/Fotolia; p. W79 Maksim Kabakou/Fotolia; p. W88 (top left) Asia Selects RF/Getty Images, (top right) UpperCut Images/Alamy, (bottom left) Bill Noll/F+/Getty Images, (bottom right) bikeriderlondon/Shutterstock; p. W89 Michael Cohen/Getty Images.

ABOUT THE AUTHORS

Joan Saslow

Joan Saslow has taught in a variety of programs in South America and the United States. She is author or coauthor of a number of widely used courses, some of which are *Ready to Go*, *Workplace Plus*, *Literacy Plus*, and *Summit*. She is also author of *English in Context*, a series for reading science and technology. Ms. Saslow was the series director of *True Colors* and *True Voices*. She has participated in the English Language Specialist Program in the U.S. Department of State's Bureau of Educational and Cultural Affairs.

Allen Ascher

Allen Ascher has been a teacher and teacher trainer in China and the United States, as well as academic director of the intensive English program at Hunter College. Mr. Ascher has also been an ELT publisher and was responsible for publication and expansion of numerous well-known courses including *True Colors*, *NorthStar*, the *Longman TOEFL Preparation Series*, and the *Longman Academic Writing Series*. He is coauthor of *Summit*, and he wrote the "Teaching Speaking" module of *Teacher Development Interactive*, an online multimedia teacher-training program.

Ms. Saslow and Mr. Ascher are frequent presenters at professional conferences and have been coauthoring courses for teens, adults, and young adults since 2002.

AUTHORS' ACKNOWLEDGMENTS

The authors are indebted to these reviewers, who provided extensive and detailed feedback and suggestions for *Top Notch*, as well as the hundreds of teachers who completed surveys and participated in focus groups.

Manuel Wilson Alvarado Miles, Quito, Ecuador • **Shirley Ando,** Otemae University, Hyogo, Japan • **Vanessa de Andrade,** CCBEU Inter Americano, Curitiba, Brazil • **Miguel Arrazola,** CBA, Santa Cruz, Bolivia • **Mark Barta,** Proficiency School of English, São Paulo, Brazil • **Edwin Bello,** PROULEX, Guadalajara, Mexico • **Mary Blum,** CBA, Cochabamba, Bolivia • **María Elizabeth Boccia,** Proficiency School of English, São Paulo, Brazil • **Pamela Cristina Borja Baltán,** Quito, Ecuador • **Eliana Anabel L. Buccia,** AMICANA, Mendoza, Argentina • **José Humberto Calderón Díaz,** CALUSAC, Guatemala City, Guatemala • **María Teresa Calienes Csirke,** Idiomas Católica, Lima, Peru • **Esther María Carbo Morales,** Quito, Ecuador • **Jorge Washington Cárdenas Castillo,** Quito, Ecuador • **Eréndira Yadira Carrera García,** UVM Chapultepec, Mexico City, Mexico • **Viviane de Cássia Santos Carlini,** Spectrum Line, Pouso Alegre, Brazil • **Centro Colombo Americano,** Bogota, Colombia • **Guven Ciftci,** Fatih University, Istanbul, Turkey • **Diego Cisneros,** CBA, Tarija, Bolivia • **Paul Crook,** Meisei University, Tokyo, Japan • **Alejandra Díaz Loo,** El Cultural, Arequipa, Peru • **Jesús G. Díaz Osío,** Florida National College, Miami, USA • **María Eid Ceneviva,** CBA, Bolivia • **Amalia Elvira Rodríguez Espinoza De Los Monteros,** Guayaquil, Ecuador • **María Argelia Estrada Vásquez,** CALUSAC, Guatemala City, Guatemala • **John Fieldeldy,** College of Engineering, Nihon University, Aizuwakamatsu-shi, Japan • **Marleni Humbelina Flores Urízar,** CALUSAC, Guatemala City, Guatemala • **Gonzalo Fortune,** CBA, Sucre, Bolivia • **Andrea Fredricks,** Embassy CES, San Francisco, USA • **Irma Gallegos Peláez,** UVM Tlalpan, Mexico City, Mexico • **Alberto Gamarra,** CBA, Santa Cruz, Bolivia • **María Amparo García Peña,** ICPNA Cusco, Peru • **Amanda Gillis-Furutaka,** Kyoto Sangyo University, Kyoto, Japan • **Martha Angelina González Párraga,** Guayaquil, Ecuador • **Octavio Garduño Ruiz,** Business Training Consultant, Mexico City, Mexico • **Ralph Grayson,** Idiomas Católica, Lima, Peru • **Murat Gultekin,** Fatih University, Istanbul, Turkey • **Oswaldo Gutiérrez,** PROULEX, Guadalajara, Mexico • **Ayaka Hashinishi,** Otemae University, Hyogo, Japan • **Alma Lorena Hernández de Armas,** CALUSAC, Guatemala City, Guatemala • **Kent Hill,** Seigakuin University, Saitama-ken, Japan • **Kayoko Hirao,** Nichii Gakkan Company, COCO Juku, Japan • **Jesse Huang,** National Central University, Taoyuan, Taiwan • **Eric Charles Jones,** Seoul University of Technology, Seoul, South Korea • **Jun-Chen Kuo,** Tajen University, Pingtung , Taiwan • **Susan Krieger,** Embassy CES, San Francisco, USA • **Ana María de la Torre Ugarte,** ICPNA Chiclayo, Peru • **Erin Lemaistre,** Chung-Ang University, Seoul, South Korea • **Eleanor S. Leu,** Soochow University, Taipei, Taiwan • **Yihui Li (Stella Li),** Fooyin University, Kaohsiung, Taiwan • **Chin-Fan Lin,** Shih Hsin University, Taipei, Taiwan • **Linda Lin,** Tatung Institute of Technology, Taiwan • **Kristen Lindblom,** Embassy CES, San Francisco, USA • **Patricio David López Logacho,** Quito, Ecuador • **Diego López Tasara,** Idiomas Católica, Lima, Peru • **Neil Macleod,** Kansai Gaidai University, Osaka, Japan • **Adriana Marcés,** Idiomas Católica, Lima, Peru • **Robyn McMurray,** Pusan National University, Busan, South Korea • **Paula Medina,** London Language Institute, London, Canada • **Juan Carlos Muñoz,** American School Way, Bogota, Colombia • **Noriko Mori,** Otemae University, Hyogo, Japan • **Adrián Esteban Narváez Pacheco,** Cuenca, Ecuador • **Tim Newfields,** Tokyo University Faculty of Economics, Tokyo, Japan • **Ana Cristina Ochoa,** CCBEU Inter Americano, Curitiba, Brazil • **Tania Elizabeth Ortega Santacruz,** Cuenca, Ecuador • **Martha Patricia Páez,** Quito, Ecuador • **María de Lourdes Pérez Valdespino,** Universidad del Valle de México, Mexico • **Wahrena Elizabeth Pfeister,** University of Suwon, Gyeonggi-Do, South Korea • **Wayne Allen Pfeister,** University of Suwon, Gyeonggi-Do, South Korea • **Andrea Rebonato,** CCBEU Inter Americano, Curitiba, Brazil • **Thomas Robb,** Kyoto Sangyo University, Kyoto, Japan • **Mehran Sabet,** Seigakuin University, Saitama-ken, Japan • **Majid Safadaran Mosazadeh,** ICPNA Chiclayo, Peru • **Timothy Samuelson,** BridgeEnglish, Denver, USA • **Héctor Sánchez,** PROULEX, Guadalajara, Mexico • **Mónica Alexandra Sánchez Escalante,** Quito, Ecuador • **Jorge Mauricio Sánchez Montalván,** Quito, Universidad Politécnica Salesiana (UPS), Ecuador • **Letícia Santos,** ICBEU Ibiá, Brazil • **Elena Sapp,** INTO Oregon State University, Corvallis, USA • **Robert Sheridan,** Otemae University, Hyogo, Japan • **John Eric Sherman,** Hong Ik University, Seoul, South Korea • **Brooks Slaybaugh,** Asia University, Tokyo, Japan • **João Vitor Soares,** NACC, São Paulo, Brazil • **Silvia Solares,** CBA, Sucre, Bolivia • **Chayawan Sonchaeng,** Delaware County Community College, Media, PA • **María Julia Suárez,** CBA, Cochabamba, Bolivia • **Elena Sudakova,** English Language Center, Kiev, Ukraine • **Richard Swingle,** Kansai Gaidai College, Osaka, Japan • **Blanca Luz Terrazas Zamora,** ICPNA Cusco, Peru • **Sandrine Ting,** St. John's University, New Taipei City, Taiwan • **Christian Juan Torres Medina,** Guayaquil, Ecuador • **Raquel Torrico,** CBA, Sucre, Bolivia • **Jessica Ueno,** Otemae University, Hyogo, Japan • **Ximena Vacaflor C.,** CBA, Tarija, Bolivia • **René Valdivia Pereira,** CBA, Santa Cruz, Bolivia • **Solange Lopes Vinagre Costa,** SENAC, São Paulo, Brazil • **Magno Alejandro Vivar Hurtado,** Cuenca, Ecuador • **Dr. Wen-hsien Yang,** National Kaohsiung Hospitality College, Kaohsiung, Taiwan • **Juan Zárate,** El Cultural, Arequipa, Peru